LONDON

The Heartless City

David Wilcox has been writing about London planning for the last eight years. He joined the *Evening Standard* in 1969 – after three years with the Reading *Evening Post* – when the debate on London's future began to hit the headlines. Motorway plans, the fate of historic buildings, hotel and office development, the decline of Docklands and the lack of coherent official policies to tackle housing problems were all issues he covered in the *Standard,* and on radio and television.

David Richards qualified as a Barrister in 1972 and later specialised in planning law.

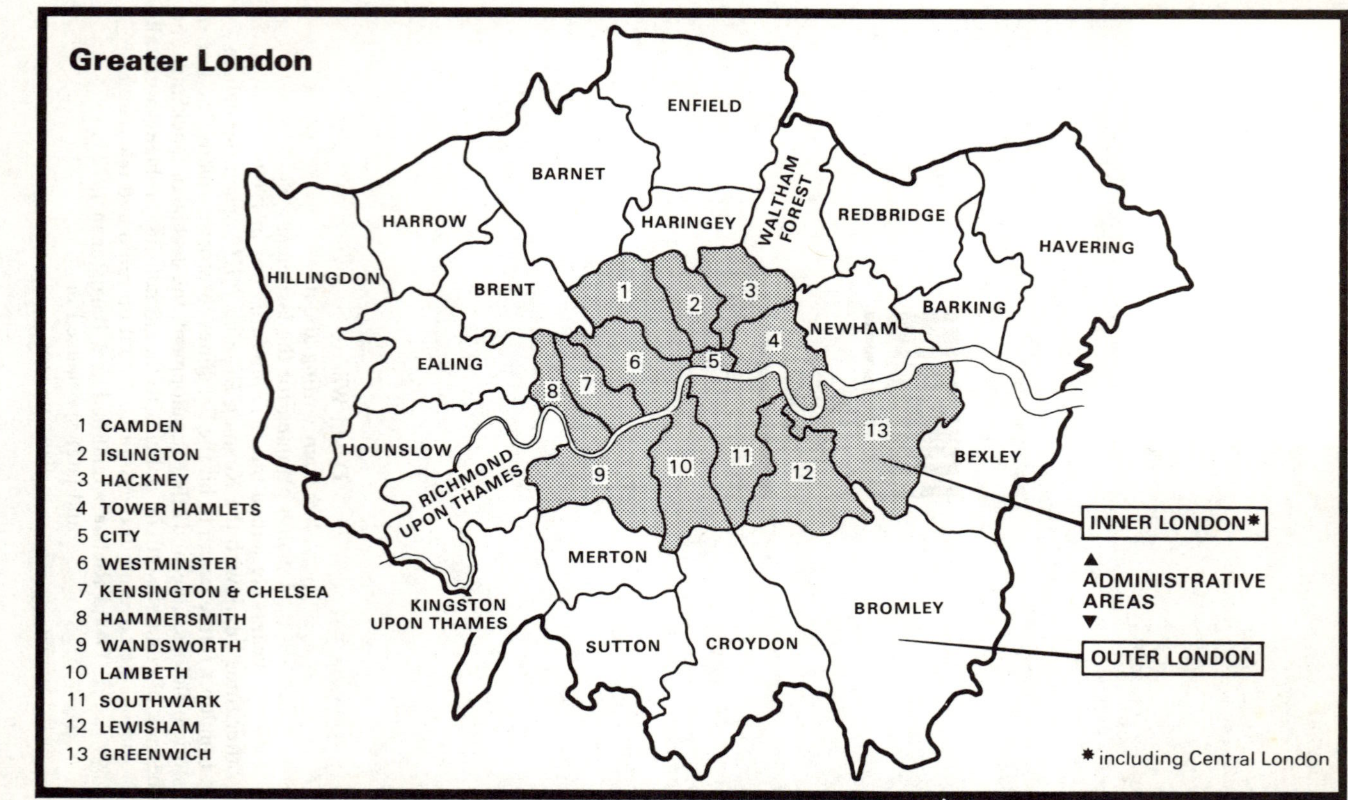

Greater London
ENFIELD
BARNET
HARROW
HARINGEY
WALTHAM FOREST
REDBRIDGE
HAVERING
HILLINGDON
BRENT
BARKING
NEWHAM
EALING
HOUNSLOW
RICHMOND UPON THAMES
BEXLEY
KINGSTON UPON THAMES
MERTON
SUTTON
CROYDON
BROMLEY
INNER LONDON*
ADMINISTRATIVE AREAS
OUTER LONDON
1 CAMDEN
2 ISLINGTON
3 HACKNEY
4 TOWER HAMLETS
5 CITY
6 WESTMINSTER
7 KENSINGTON & CHELSEA
8 HAMMERSMITH
9 WANDSWORTH
10 LAMBETH
11 SOUTHWARK
12 LEWISHAM
13 GREENWICH
* including Central London

LONDON

The Heartless City

David Wilcox
with David Richards

First published by Thames Television 1977
306 Euston Road London NW1 3BB

Distributed by Argus Books Limited
14 St James Road Watford Herts

ISBN 0 85242 554 6

Printed in Great Britain by Macdermott & Chant Limited

Cartography: Richard Natkiel
Cover design: Ken Briggs
Typography: Helen Lindon

This book was commissioned by Thames Television as a contribution to its *London Looks Forward* project. The views expressed are those of the authors.

CONTENTS

Foreword	7
Introduction	11
Planning and Politics	17
Earning a Living	34
Moving Around the City	51
Finding a Home	79
The Three-ring City	97
Living in London	125
Manifesto for London	161
Acknowledgments	171

FOREWORD

This is a book about London's immediate past and future, written and published in the space of less than six months in Jubilee Year 1977. It is written by a former *Evening Standard* journalist, and it is commissioned and published by Thames, one of London's independent television stations. It is a report to Londoners on the state of their city, seen through the eyes of one of them, and drawing on scores of interviews with those who guard its fortunes and grapple with its problems.

It is not a comfortable book to read. Anyone expecting uplift or optimism should stop here. But neither is it a story of unrelieved gloom. It is a very honest book, and a very penetrating one. It shows London as it is, at the beginning of the last quarter of the twentieth century. It depicts a city that, contrary to the popular vision of many, is actually in a state of decline. It chronicles a sad story of muddle and indecision and delay on the part of those responsible for London's government. It suggests strongly that many key policies, still in operation, may be positively perverse in that they are doing London, and Londoners, actual injury.

So it will excite intense controversy. And that, in a Greater London election year, is entirely proper. It may even encourage Londoners to start thinking about new policy bundles that would be consistent, and that would be helpful rather than harmful.

The key facts are not in doubt. London – that is Greater London – has lost one and a half million people since its 1939 peak. If trends continue, by 1990 it will have lost more than a million more. In the last decade and a half, it has lost half a million jobs; that trend, too, is expected to continue. Among certain groups, such as West Indian youth, unemployment may be as high as 30 per cent. There are still tens of thousands of families caught in a trap of poor housing, poor job prospects, low income, inadequate skills and limited prospects for their children. The costs of vital public services, above all public transport, continue to soar; if fares rise to cover them people will no longer be able to afford to travel, but if they are subsidised from the rates then people may react by voting with their feet. In a new poll, quoted here for the first time, more than half of all Londoners say they would like to move because they dislike their neighbourhood.

Yet it is not all a story of disaster. Many Londoners still do like their city – including the new arrivals drawn by its opportunities. Tourists from all over the world flock to it in increasing numbers, to provide the base of what is now probably London's major industry. London is still indisputably a centre for finance, for the media, for entertainment – in short, nearly all the fastest growing tertiary industries – without rival in Europe, and with few rivals in the world. Despite everything, its quality of life is felt by many to be superior to that of other world cities.

The fact is that, like any great city at any time, London now is in a state of flux. It has strengths and weaknesses. Certain activities grow; others decline. Some kinds of people arrive; others, for equally good reasons, leave. The physical fabric of the city alters to accommodate new jobs, new homes. In the classical economist's mythical market, all these adjustments might be performed more or less painlessly through a myriad of individual decisions. But we have long ceased to believe that this is entirely possible or desirable, and so we invoke planning to help us order and guide the process of change.

Here, though, is the nub of the problem. From Wilcox's detailed analyses, it seems that too often planning has performed this role clumsily, ponderously, and illogically. It has shut down factories as part of redevelopment plans, while resisting proposals for offices and shops and showrooms that might have provided alternative jobs; it has exported factory jobs to the Assisted Areas, and office jobs to towns like Reading and Southend, while employment opportunities in London were contracting. It has systematically squeezed the private landlord who alone can provide the vital flexibility that a great city's housing market must have – particularly in catering for the first time entrant; it has restricted its poorest citizens' chances to move out to decent housing in new towns. It has abandoned road plans that might have attracted new industry, but has allowed public transport fares to rise to a point where they threaten the viability of central London as an employment centre. It has gone round in circles on vital questions of redevelopment or renewal, appearing to bend in the wind before each successive well-organised pressure group.

Above all, in general it appears to have been amazingly myopic. It ran after fashionable hares – decongest London, fight speculators, conserve the fabric, protect public transport – rather than making a deep analysis of London's problems and the alternative ways of solving them. Presumably this was not due to lack of qualified analysts, because (as Wilcox shows) one London mystery is the vast size of the County Hall establishment. Rather, it seems to be because the politicians pursued whatever gimmick was fashionable and might win some easy votes.

What lines would such an analysis take? It would have to start from the brutal fact that London, and Londoners, have to make a living; in the present economic state of Great Britain, there are all too few other people or places who might be called upon to subsidise it. It will make this living by doing what it can do well, and competitively. That probably means more tertiary industry, and less manufacturing – though some kinds of factory industry will flourish there, as they always have. It means more offices and hotels and conference centres and marinas and possibly even a Disneyland – perhaps in the heart of the Docklands. And it means training, and retraining, to put ex-dockers and unemployed West Indian youths into the new jobs that these will bring.

It also means a housing policy that accepts the principle of subsidy, but uses it to help those who need it most; and that, above all, provides sufficient flexibility so that people have some access to housing. It may mean students in local authority tower blocks, council housing at market rents for secretaries who can afford it, and a determined drive to help lower income people go to the new and expanded towns – where, as recent research has clearly shown, a substantial minority would be happy to move.

It means a selective redevelopment policy that provides well designed new offices and shops and showrooms in the places that could take them – especially around major railway stations. It means a transport policy that eschews grandiose and ill-conceived investments like the £200 million River Line, and instead concentrates on schemes that will tempt industry back and cater for the hard pressed commuter.

Above all, it means a recognition that in the last resort, it does not matter whether London is half a million people less or more. What does matter is that its people, whatever their number, have interesting work that brings an adequate income; access to the housing market, not just in their local borough's bailiwick, but embracing all London and extending to the new and expanded towns; a quality of life that satisfies them. The problem of London is not those who have left, but those that remain and are dissatisfied with their lot.

London can thrive and it can be greater – in a qualitative, not a quantitative, sense. That is the message of this book. But it will demand greater honesty in facing the facts, and greater breadth of vision, than the politicians and the officials have given us in the past. This book is a crucial pointer in that direction.

Peter Hall

Professor of Geography, University of Reading

INTRODUCTION

More than half the people living in London would like to move out because they do not like their neighbourhood. A national survey carried out for Thames Television by Research Surveys of Great Britain showed that this astonishing level of disgruntlement was not due to depression brought on by living through a slump, nor to a natural feeling that the grass is greener elsewhere. For while fifty-two per cent of Londoners want to move, only twenty-eight per cent of those questioned elsewhere in the country were similarly restless. Londoners are quite clear where they would like to live when they do move: somewhere away from the centre. The strongest preference was for a town not too far from the capital (thirty-three per cent), next came the suburbs (thirty per cent) and then the countryside (sixteen per cent). Only five per cent said they would like to live in central London. All this could be construed as another set of doom-laden statistics to add to the file-filled cupboards of County Hall. But this file accords with reality: because people in London do not simply think about moving. Those who can move out actually do so, in their hundreds of thousands.

By the time today's five-year-olds are having their first children, London's population is expected to have dropped by about one million. In inner London those children will be among only 226,000 in schools, instead of the 360,000 of their parents' day. The number of jobs in the capital will probably have fallen by 400,000. This will be largely the result of a continuing trend for people and firms to move away from the centre to the suburbs, and out beyond the Green Belt.

Dispersal from the heart of London has provoked frightened cries about decline and decay. Comparisons with American cities have been invoked: economic collapse and urban uncontrollability; the affluent suburbs of fenced estates protected by armed guards, with little public transport; the inner areas racked by crime and violence, their poverty-trapped inhabitants ill-catered for by over-stretched welfare services.

True, the capital is spreading into the Home Counties and growth in the South East as a whole has stopped. But it does not follow that the result must be dereliction and disaster for London. The movement outwards can have beneficial as well as adverse effects: fewer people in the city means less congestion on the roads, smaller classes in schools, a larger choice of housing. With greater car ownership, most journeys in the outer London of the 1990s will be by personal rather than public transport. With fewer jobs in the centre of London, the crush of commuting will be reduced considerably, because instead of catching the 8.14 to Waterloo, Dorking man will drive to his job in Windsor.

This book does not try to forecast what the London of the 1990s will be like. That will depend upon Britain's economic performance in the world, the aspirations of the next generation, and a host of other factors which are beyond the control of Government and defy prediction. Instead it attempts to describe how, in those areas which most directly affect our everyday lives, central and local Government have worked either with or against the economic and social changes which are taking place. In particular it is about the way politicians, planners, journalists and pressure groups can unwittingly conspire to produce the wrong policies and panaceas. All too often those trends which could bring benefits are countered, while those which precipitate problems are encouraged. Somehow the pendulum of fashion swings too fast. One year hotels are ruining the West End, the next year we desperately need more hotel beds for the vital tourist industry. New roads are seen as a major threat to the urban environment, then suddenly as the only way to attract industry back to areas of high unemployment. In the early 1970s, councils were lambasted for failing to employ enough social workers, subsidise fares, build homes. In 1977 they are castigated for overstaffing and rate rises.

There is no consistent vision of the role of a capital city, not least because London's government has been designed to ensure that political control is frequently split. Three masters control London's housing, planning and transport: central Government, the Greater London Council (GLC) and local borough councils. Even when they are of the same political complexion, the three tiers squabble over who does what. When they are different, they feel obliged to act out pale reflections of Westminster's political rows. No system could be better designed in the name of democracy to ensure that no-one can actually take a decision and carry it through. If a Labour GLC decides to build council houses in the suburbs, a Tory borough will block them. If a Tory borough decides to give planning permission for an office block, Labour in County Hall will turn it down. If a Labour GLC decides to subsidise fares heavily, Government of any political hue will insist instead that public expenditure is cut, and fares raised.

The arguments are bread and butter for journalists, a fertile field for community associations skilled at playing one body off against another. Thousands of council officers and civil servants are engaged at great expense in the task of producing mountains of reports to justify sincerely-held political postures.

However, most Londoners are totally indifferent to the games played out in their name. They want the obvious necessities of urban life – efficient transport, a reasonable choice of housing, clean streets, safe neighbourhoods, good schools – but they do not know which party is capable of providing these services at local level. Instead, they vote on national political lines at local borough and GLC elections. Since these elections are held in different years, it is almost certain that the changing fortunes of national political parties will ensure a division of responsibility.

The response of the weary ratepayer to this charade is often to cry that politics should be taken out of local government. But that is impossible, and probably undesirable. Local government decisions on who gets the best housing and transport, the quietest streets, best social services or lowest rates are by their nature intensely political. Decisions by councils on whether to build houses or sell them off, to buy out landlords or encourage home ownership, will influence which groups of people, rich or poor, shall live in London. Building roads or subsidising public transport will help determine which firms shall find it easiest to recruit commuters or get lorries through the London traffic jams to the ports and export markets. Indeed, while all policies are political it is not always easy to tag them with a recognisable party colour. Politicians have jumped on policies in an attempt to ride the swing of fashion, only to abandon them once the pendulum has reversed and the damage is done.

It is easy to blame politicians, council officers and civil servants for our grievances. But usually their policies represent the fossilised embodiment of changing public whims. Voters endorse manifesto pledges which are then turned into legislation and administered by officials; if the rules and regulations are irksome, we must bear some of the responsibility. The first chapter of this book sets out the formal basis on which London should in theory be governed, and looks at the grand plans which have attempted to put some order on the mass of individual aspirations which shape towns and cities. In the 1940s, it all seemed relatively simple. London was overcrowded, and noxious industry was mixed with bad housing: why not move out the many who would be glad to go, leaving space for planned rebuilding of homes and factories? Thirty years later, millions of people would still like to leave London, and many do; but the pendulum of concern has swung back. There is anxiety that Government is spending too much on the New Towns and not enough on derelict Dockland and the remainder of the inner city – and that London is losing its most enterprising firms and ablest workers.

Yet London is spreading out whether the planners like it or not. Over the past thirty years, for a variety of reasons, industry has moved from inner London to the suburbs and beyond, or died on the spot. Sites for expansion have always been cheaper and easier to develop away from the centre; transport is better and skilled labour easier to recruit. Government has encouraged decentralisation and local councils have knocked down back street workshops. Since the 1960s, offices have been following industry for similar reasons, even though the demand for prestige central London accommodation as headquarters for large firms has created an impression of growth in the City and West End. But even before the firms themselves moved out, their employees were departing for the suburbs, and even further afield, as better transport made it easy to buy a place of one's own on the edge of the city while keeping a well paid job.

At first, office workers commuted back into town; but as jobs decentralised a fundamental change has taken place. Those who moved out have bought cars, and many have found it far more convenient to drive from Camberley to Croydon, or Bracknell to Heathrow in order to work. Statistics show fewer and fewer people commuting into central London, and more and more driving around or in and out of the edge of London. The old image of a congested central London putting out tentacles along its rail lines to the suburbs is now less appropriate. It must be supplemented with the picture of a 'ring city' developing around the edge of Greater London. In this ring city, most people do not rely on the centre for their jobs or their entertainment, nor for any other personal or social service. For them the centre may as well not exist. But as the healthy organism grows on the perimeter, so the heart decays.

So far, the Labour GLC has reacted with total inconsistency to this trend and Tories have failed to come to terms with it. Labour politicians have deplored the loss of people and jobs from the inner city while curbing central office development there and encouraging development of strategic centres in the suburbs. They have endorsed the M25 ring road outside London, while abandoning roads within the city. By inhibiting owner-occupation and favouring council housing, they have ensured that the one place where skilled workers can fulfil their ambition to own a home is outside London rather than inside. And they have made little provision for the young and single who actually want to move into central London. The Tories have promised to tackle inner city problems but refuse to endorse council housing in the suburbs, thus preventing the poorer and less skilled from escaping the inner city to some prospect of work near the industry which has moved out.

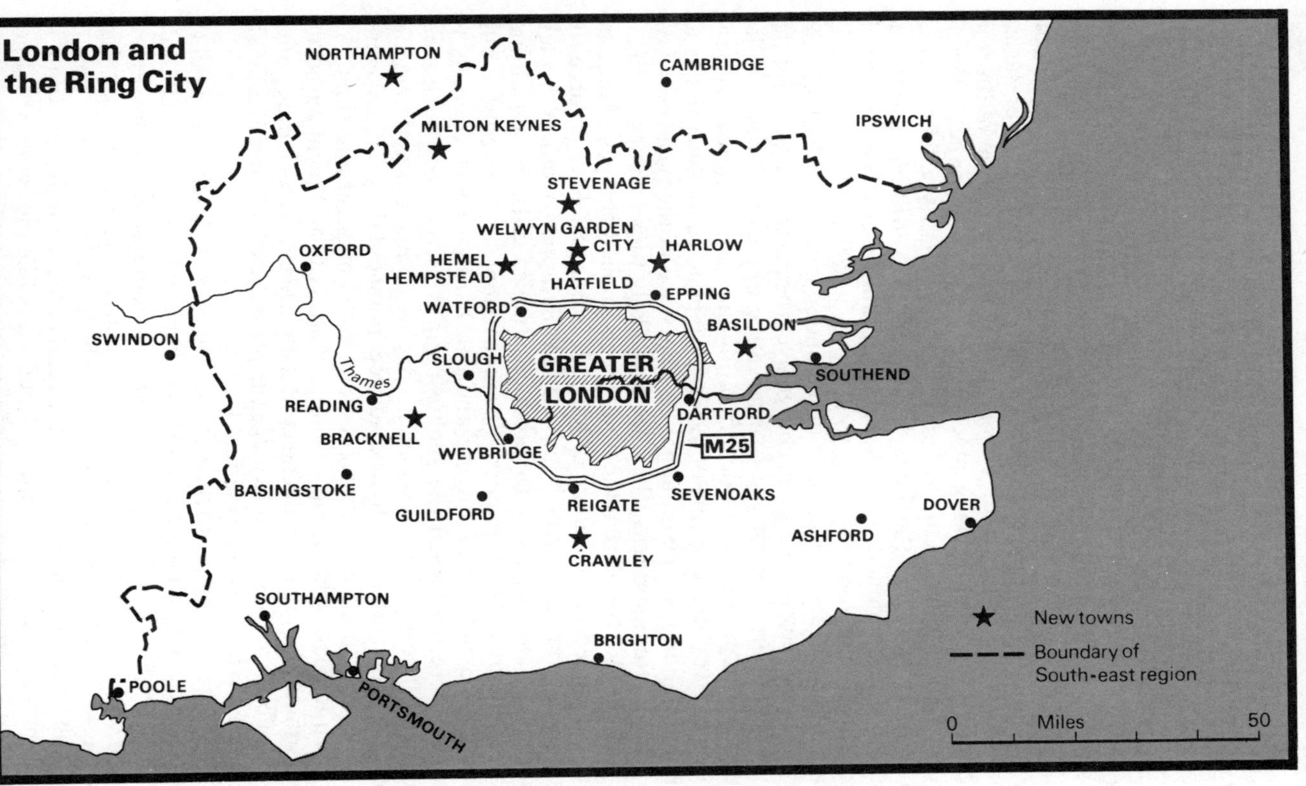
London and the Ring City
NORTHAMPTON
CAMBRIDGE
IPSWICH
MILTON KEYNES
STEVENAGE
WELWYN GARDEN CITY
HARLOW
OXFORD
HEMEL HEMPSTEAD
HATFIELD
EPPING
WATFORD
BASILDON
SWINDON
SLOUGH
GREATER LONDON
SOUTHEND
Thames
READING
DARTFORD
BRACKNELL
M25
WEYBRIDGE
BASINGSTOKE
SEVENOAKS
GUILDFORD
REIGATE
DOVER
ASHFORD
CRAWLEY
SOUTHAMPTON
New towns
BRIGHTON
Boundary of South-east region
POOLE
PORTSMOUTH
0
Miles
50

Throughout the book there are a large number of references to the GLC and fewer to the boroughs. This does not reflect the relative status of those two tiers of government: indeed, a widely held view is that the boroughs are generally credible organisations while the GLC has failed to fulfil the strategic role envisaged when it was created in 1964. The reason for the disproportionate treatment here is that this book is about strategic rather than local issues and this is the area for which the GLC should be responsible. Equally, because I have tried to avoid abstract debate by using real examples, there is some concentration on the apparent failure of many GLC policies over the last four years of Labour rule. This is merely an illustration of the way London's decision-making machinery works – or rather, doesn't work. Labour policies of 1973 and 1974 were a fairly valid reflection of majority opinion of the times. Many have proved inappropriate and have been abandoned with changing circumstances. The trouble is that the change took too long to achieve, and few positive policies have emerged. Labour policies come under scrutiny and attack simply because they have been in charge over the past few years. But this implies no partiality for the Conservative opposition, which failed singularly to perform its critical function until an election was on the horizon. Even in the spring of 1977, Tory policies looked thin: as an administration their claim might be that since in the past they have generally attempted less, they are less likely to get things wrong.

It might also be felt that the book levels implied charges of bureaucratic bumbledom at council officers. It is impossible to divorce the individual from the organisation: we are all trapped in our own roles. Journalists are expected to produce simple, critical, sensational stories which sell newspapers. To some extent, they invent the officials they delight in parodying and can hardly expect councils to display more flair when the slightest slip is seized upon with glee. Council officers, many of whom are highly competent and imaginative, are expected to weigh the evidence, point out the problems – and to protect their political masters from such embarrassing slips.

Even insiders who argue privately that GLC and local authority staffs should be greatly reduced (and there are many, including politicians of both parties) acknowledge the pressures that council officials undergo in the cause of political face-saving.

Nevertheless, since officials are paid to serve politicians and politicians are elected or nominated to serve the electorate, it is to all three in their respective roles that this book is addressed. Its message is that in far too many cases the system of planning and government has not worked, and is not working, for the benefit of Londoners. That *is* the fault of council officials. It *is* the fault of local politicians. But it is much more the fault of ordinary Londoners like me, who won't get interested or angry or even hopeful about the future of their city.

PLANNING AND POLITICS

Thirty-four years ago, when London was being devastated by German bombers, a group of nine planners produced their vision of London in the future. When the rubble was cleared, large areas of East London would be rebuilt and new roads constructed; old wharves would be cleared from the south bank of the Thames and replaced by parks and playgrounds, new homes and fine civic buildings.

Introducing their County of London Plan in 1943, the Leader of the London County Council (LCC), Lord Latham, said: 'Our London has much that is lovely and gracious. I do not know that any city can rival its parks and gardens, its squares and terraces. But year by year as the nineteenth and twentieth centuries grew more and more absorbed in first gaining and then holding material prosperity, these graces were overlaid and a tide of mean, ugly, unplanned building rose in every London borough and flooded outward over the fields of Middlesex, Surrey, Essex and Kent.'

The planners, under Professor Patrick Abercrombie and LCC architect J. H. Forshaw, had spent only a year in producing their 180-page report but they were precise in their diagnosis. Inner London was suffering from traffic congestion, decayed housing, a severe lack of parks in certain areas, and homes standing side by side with factories in heavily polluted back streets. They prescribed rigid controls on development to stop further mixtures of homes and industry, action to remove existing factories from residential streets, creation of new parks and redevelopment of housing. The elbow room to create attractive new areas amid the congestion of inner London was to be found by shifting 1,033,000 Londoners and their work-places out beyond the Green Belt in a massive overspill operation.

Abercrombie specified how this overspill was to be accommodated in his complementary plan for the wider area of Greater London, which was published in 1944. The most dramatic of his proposals was the creation of ten New Towns outside the Green Belt. By 1946 the first of these, Stevenage, was already under way, and within a further four years, seven more were begun. In the 1944 plan he also tackled the problem of urban sprawl, for London was straggling out along the Great West Road and other highways. He recommended legislation to make the Green Belt inviolable.

Abercrombie's scheme to decant people and industry from London dominated the thinking of a whole generation of planners, and the main proposals of his plan were carried out. The New Towns have since housed hundreds of thousands of people and the Green Belt has restricted London's peripheral growth. There has been a great deal of redevelopment in inner London; the Royal Festival Hall, the Queen Elizabeth Hall, the Hayward Gallery and the National Theatre now form the basis of a central cultural complex on the South Bank.

Indeed, thirty-four years later a common complaint is that Abercrombie's plans for dispersal succeeded much too well. The trend he encouraged has spiralled, so that more people than he planned have already left the capital – not just for the New Towns but also for private estates beyond the Green Belt where they can buy homes with gardens for as little as £10,000. Abercrombie planned to reduce Greater London's population by just over one million, but specified no time scale. He used as a base figure the 1939 population estimate of 8,615,000. By 1960 the population had fallen below eight million and in mid-1976 it stood at seven million; it may well fall to below six million by 1991.

Today there is furious debate about the effects of decentralisation. Passionate defenders of New Towns, such as the Town and Country Planning Association, say that since people want to leave cities anyway it is best that they be encouraged to settle in properly designed environments. Both people and industry thrive in the new settlements and, furthermore, the exodus creates space in the inner areas and allows planned regeneration of the old city. Critics of the New and Expanding Towns policy claim that the great drive to decentralise people and jobs has sucked the life-blood from the inner city; that the ten per cent unemployment figure in Brixton and thirteen per cent in Stepney is due to firms having set up in Harlow, Crawley or in Milton Keynes. They maintain that it is the skilled workers and most enterprising firms who have left, not the poorer families of Tower Hamlets, Lambeth and Southwark, who most need a fresh start in life. Nor, they say, has the inner city regeneration materialised in the form envisaged.

In December 1975, the Labour controlled Greater London Council joined the critics and announced that it would reconsider agreements whereby it built homes for Londoners in the New and Expanding Towns and encouraged industry to move there. Although only a relatively small proportion of those leaving London go to the New

POPULATION CHANGES IN GREATER LONDON

Inner London	**1951**	**1961**	%	**1971**	%	**(mid) 1976**	%
Camden	258	246	−5	207	−20	186	−28
Greenwich	236	230	−3	218	−8	207	−13
Hackney	265	258	−3	220	−17	193	−27
Hammersmith	241	222	−8	187	−22	170	−29
Islington	271	261	−4	202	−25	172	−37
Kensington & Chelsea	219	219	N/C	188	−14	161	−26
Lambeth	347	342	−2	308	−11	290	−16
Lewisham	303	291	−4	268	−12	237	−22
Southwark	338	313	−7	262	−22	225	−33
Tower Hamlets	231	206	−11	166	−28	146	−37
Wandsworth	331	335	+1	302	−9	285	−14
Westminster	300	272	−9	240	−20	216	−28
City of London	5	5	N/C	4	−20	7	+40
Total	**3,345**	**3,200**	**−4**	**2,772**	**−17**	**2,495**	**−25**

Outer London	**1951**	**1961**	%	**1971**	%	**(mid) 1976**	%
Barking	189	177	−6	161	−15	154	−19
Barnet	320	318	−0.7	307	−4	305	−5
Bexley	205	210	+2	217	+6	214	+4
Brent	311	296	−5	281	−10	257	−17
Bromley	268	293	+9	305	+14	299	+12
Croydon	310	324	+5	334	+8	331	+7
Ealing	311	302	−3	301	−3	294	−5
Enfield	288	274	−5	268	−7	261	−9
Haringey	277	259	−6	240	−13	228	−18
Harrow	219	209	−5	203	−7	200	−9
Havering	192	246	+28	248	+29	239	+24
Hillingdon	210	228	+9	235	+12	231	+10
Hounslow	211	209	−1	207	−2	199	−6
Kingston upon Thames	147	146	−1	141	−4	136	−7
Morton	200	189	−5	177	−11	169	−15
Newham	294	265	−10	237	−19	229	−22
Redbridge	257	250	−3	240	−7	232	−10
Richmond upon Thames	188	181	−4	175	−7	167	−11
Sutton	176	169	−4	169	−4	167	−5
Waltham Forest	275	249	−9	235	−15	224	−19
Total	**4,848**	**4,794**	**−1**	**4,681**	**−4**	**4,536**	**−6**

Total for Greater London	**1951**	**1961**	%	**1971**	%	**(mid) 1976**	%
	8,197	**7,992**	−2.5	**7,452**	−9	**7,028**	−14

All figures rounded to nearest thousand. N/C = no change.
Percentages represent percentage change compared to 1951 population.
Sources: 1951, 1961, 1971 figures: Census data.
1976 figures: Office of Population Census and Surveys.

Towns under the planned overspill scheme, this announcement presented a severe challenge to a sacred tenet of British planning and launched a major debate on the decline of cities.

By the autumn of the following year, the issue centred on the effect of dispersal on inner city areas. The Environment Secretary, Peter Shore, made a speech in Manchester which amounted to a complete reassessment by Government of thirty years' planning. He said that the unbalanced nature of migration from the inner cities was leaving those areas with 'a disproportionate share of unskilled and semi-skilled workers, of unemployment, of one parent families, of concentrations of immigrant communities and overcrowded and inadequate housing.' He conceded that the problems had arisen partly because of planned dispersal and partly because people and firms were leaving of their own accord. Not only should the encouragement of dispersal be questioned, but so should other Abercrombie fundamentals such as the separation of housing from industry:

> There has been an assumption that people do not like workplaces in the same areas as their homes, but this is not always the case. Many people value the way in which a factory or plant can help sustain a community and the fact that they can walk or cycle to work.

Whatever Mr Shore or the GLC say, there is little they can do to halt the outflow of people and jobs, precisely because most are going to places other than the publicly built and financed New Towns. The Government and local councils could refuse to allow any more planning permissions for new private homes for emigrant Londoners in areas like booming East Berkshire, but that would do little good since many old permissions are still valid. Consequently, the debate has focussed on the continuing flow to New Towns of public finance which might otherwise be diverted to inner city areas.

Peter Shore's speech led to mounting fears among the second generation of New and Expanding Towns such as Milton Keynes, Peterborough and Northampton that they could face cuts in their budgets so that the new Cabinet Committee on inner city problems, chaired by Mr Shore, could recommend diverting resources back into the old towns and cities. The GLC, in particular, wanted one billion pounds of public money channelled over twenty years into the regeneration of 5,000 acres of Docklands in East London which had sunk into dereliction as dock trade moved down river to Tilbury. It was such claims for resources, rather than the direct effects of dispersal, that had prompted the change in policy away from New and Expanding Towns.

Rates and Responsibilities

The real issue behind the decentralisation argument comes back to precisely who goes, and who stays. The dispersal plans of the Fifties and Sixties were in operation when economic growth was encouraging expansion and the birth rate was rising. It seemed perfectly reasonable to plan major 'counter magnets' to London to house the extra population in orderly fashion and prevent the need for London to spread into the Green Belt. Only by creating growth areas like Milton Keynes, Northampton and Peterborough could the rest of the countryside be protected from unplanned sprawl. But now that growth has slowed down and the population is falling, a different picture emerges. The more dynamic firms move out to better sites where lorries can quickly feed into the motorway network. It is the old firms, which cannot get credit for expansion, that are left behind and eventually die. Office blocks are still going up, but the number of office jobs in the centre is falling as firms find that they, like industry, can operate more cheaply in the suburbs. It is their head offices which large firms want to be in grand air-conditioned accommodation in the centre, not their clerical departments. Indeed, there is now unemployment among clerical workers in central London.

This decentralisation means not only fewer jobs, but also a less valuable property base on which rates can be charged. The borough councils of the inner city, such as Wandsworth, Lambeth, Tower Hamlets and Islington, find that as the commercial activity in their areas lessens, the residents have to bear more of the rates burden. The rateable value of London as a whole (currently £1,866 million) is falling by about 0.4 per cent a year, while nationally rateable value is rising by about one per cent. This means that London – and particularly inner London – has a falling tax-base with which to pay for social and environmental programmes.

Extra Government grants compensate in part for the loss of rateable value. So does the system for spreading the load around London: rich authorities like the City, with rateable values of over £200 million, and Westminster with rateable values of over £300 million, help out the poorer councils. Despite this extra help, it can be argued that London is suffering. In 1976/77, for example, the London resident paid £148 in rates, compared with an average payment of £93 in the rest of England and Wales. Since London earnings were only some fifteen per cent higher in 1975, the London councils are perhaps justified in complaining. They argue that they should be getting an extra £145 million on their grant of about £910 million in 1976/7 to bring rates more in line with the national average. No wonder people are moving out of town, they grumble. The problem is that if London is to get more, other parts of the country must get less. Already, Government moves to give more help to the cities have brought howls of outrage from county councils, and protests that they are having to cut their services.

DISTRIBUTION OF RATES ALLOCATED TO PUBLIC SERVICES IN GREATER LONDON

	%
Education	34.33
Housing	20.98
Police	9.43
Personal Social Services	9.36
Highways	4.89
Trading (cemeteries, etc)	4.19
Parks, Open Spaces	2.10
Fire	1.91
Refuse Collection	1.75
Libraries, Museums and Art Galleries	1.64
T and C Planning	1.47
Other Public Health	1.22
Baths and Indoor sports	0.86
Waste Disposal	0.78
Other Services	5.05

Source: Return of rates: Estimated expenditure 1975/6.

It would be logical to assume that as the number of people in London falls, so should the costs of looking after them: fewer children in schools, not so many clients for social workers, shorter housing waiting lists and less competition to buy or rent property. The price of land should drop, so making it easier and cheaper to build homes with gardens, and to lay out parks. But this does not happen. Land prices remain high. One explanation is that councils, housing associations and other public bodies are still buying and keeping prices up. Another is that land holdings are such a major part of investment portfolios that all institutions want to see them maintained. It is union pension funds as much as private landowners that benefit from high land values.

The cost of developing the land is also high. Basements have to be filled; old sewers and gas and water pipes must be dug up and replaced; wages for building workers are higher in London; sites are cramped and need special equipment. Few firms want to build new factories, and few private developers want to use the site of an old paint factory or railway siding for a housing estate. High development costs and a general air of dilapidation also discourage complementary private investment in clothes shops, cafes, chemists and supermarkets; for if no offices are built, there will be no extra customers to provide those shops with a satisfactory turnover.

Private affluence – Public squalor

Areas where there are more old age pensioners and single parent families, and where incomes are generally lower, do not boast many restaurants, delicatessens, freezer shops, theatres, boutiques, bookshops or travel agents. They lack banks and post offices, but have an abundance of bingo halls and Chinese take-away food shops. Services such as a good range of solicitors, accountants or a thriving doctors' group practice may also be missing. None of this may matter much to staunch defenders of the working-class lifestyle of the last generation, but all the evidence of market research is that the current generation, whatever their class background, tends to have the same material aspirations. If they cannot find the shops and amenities they want in Hackney, they will leave for the suburbs where they can buy a house and a car, drive the kids to school and shop at the new shopping centre or the bulk-buying warehouse with a large car park.

Caught in the midst of this depressing diagnosis of the urban condition, decision makers find they can do nothing right. They are attacked for being too successful in dispersing people to the New Towns. On the other hand, whenever they encourage private investment, they are criticised for destroying the environment or favouring the middle classes. For some seven or eight years, for example, planners have been criticised for building shopping centres with car parks on the grounds that this favours car owners and drains trade away from traditional shopping high streets. Nor, say the critics, should they allow the middle classes to 'gentrify' working class areas. Comprehensive redevelopment of areas such as Clapham Junction and Ealing is considered destructive of the delicate balance of old shops and small firms. Exhibition and conference centres, trade marts and super funfairs – all projects in which developers have been interested in investing private funds – have been opposed by trades councils and amenity societies. Some of the proposals were, indeed, highly destructive and rightly squashed. But without some such changes people and firms will leave London for places which do adapt to their demands.

The planner is faced with a dilemma. In places such as Docklands, where he would like some investment, he cannot attract private money because wealth and skill do not exist there already, so there is not enough potential return. Developers are not interested unless roads and rail links are built, sewers laid and sites cleared. Yet there is not much prospect of this public finance unless some is diverted from, say, the New Towns. On the other hand, whenever the planner swings with the market, allows an office block or hotel, or proposes building homes for sale instead of council housing, he is accused of increasing the polarity of benefits between rich and poor, favouring the speculator and neglecting the interests of the ordinary Londoner. It is not much help to say simply that this is the fault of the capitalist system, unless you are prepared to tread the revolutionary road that leads to total planning. But some better system of decision-making is surely needed. Under the present political system, decisions are often taken on the undemocratic vote of whichever group shouts the loudest. Schemes such as a third London airport at Maplin or the Channel Tunnel which, through their rail and road links to London, might have provided more jobs, were scrapped by Government as much because of protests from conservation groups as through lack of finance. Even the expansion of Heathrow, which would give a boost to West London, is considered doubtful because of increased aircraft noise. Residents' views are quite properly respected, but at the expense of those who would get new jobs at the airport.

One might have expected the Greater London Development Plan (GLDP) to have provided the means of resolving some of these questions. After all, it had been ten years in gestation. The GLC started work on the plan in April 1965, it was published in 1969, and the public inquiry lasted from July 1970 until May 1972. The Department of the Environment considered the plan from early 1973 – when the report of the Panel of Inquiry under Frank Layfield was submitted – until July 1976 when it was published as the Modified Plan. Yet it was notable in arousing almost no public interest.

It would be unjust to cast upon the GLC or the Department of the Environment all the blame for the slow production and ineffective nature of the plan. The approach to planning has changed since the 1940s; in his plans, Abercrombie not only covered strategic policy and details of implementation, but also identified the end-state that he envisaged. Planners are no longer so comprehensive and precise in their approach. The content of the Greater London Development Plan is regulated by the Town & Country Planning Act of 1968 and by the London Government Act of 1963 which provides that the GLDP should 'lay down considerations of general policy with respect to the use of land . . . in Greater London including, in particular, guidance as to the future road system'.

The function of the Greater London Development Plan was merely to set out guidelines which provide a framework for policy decisions. It was considered inappropriate, as well as impracticable, for the GLC to cover both strategic policy and implementation because much of what happens to London is the result of actions and events beyond the control of government, central and local. Abercrombie was planning at a time when New Towns and much other development were to be carried out by public bodies with public funds. Now, the demand for offices and factories is greatly dependent on the state of the national economy, which is more sensitive to a war in the Middle East than a change of occupant in County Hall, or even Downing Street. The changed approach amongst planners recognises that, for instance, the demand for private houses depends on the flow of mortgage funds which is in turn governed by national and international interest rates. And it is individuals, not governments, who decide whether to buy cars or travel by public transport, and whether to have babies and move to the suburbs or stay single and live in Earls Court.

The planners may draw up schemes for the future, but most of the implementation has to be done by firms and individuals who pay more attention to economic circumstances than a theoretical blueprint. The planners find their only power is to say no; or, yes, provided you carry out our plan for us. Their role is more often negative than positive.

The nature and structure of local government, and the political climate in which decisions are taken, have also changed since the 1940s. Abercrombie was acting in a purely advisory capacity, at the direct request of the government. He was able to recommend what he thought was best; he was a planner, not a politician. In addition, the Government was able to carry out Abercrombie's proposals more easily than could its modern counterpart because in the 1940s, smaller local authorities were relatively powerless. The only effective opposition might have come from the London County Council, but their chief architect, J. H. Forshaw, was a joint author with Abercrombie on the County of London Plan, 1943. In preparing the current Greater London Development Plan, the GLC had to tread more carefully. Although the permanent officers did the work, ultimate responsibility for the plan falls upon the shoulders of its politicians, acting through council committees. County Hall politicians are more sensitive to the demands and pressures of other local authorities than was Abercrombie, for the boroughs are much more powerful than they were in the 1940s.

Governing London

Until 1965, inner London was governed by the London County Council, established in 1889 and run with an iron hand by Labour politicians such as Herbert Morrison and Ike Hayward. Within the LCC area were twenty-eight metropolitan boroughs and the City. Outer London as we now know it was administered by Surrey, Kent, Middlesex, Hertfordshire and Essex, with district councils as the lower-tier authorities and also by county boroughs of Croydon, East and West Ham. In all, there were 117 local government units in London and it was unmanageable. The Herbert Commission, set up in 1957 to advise on the rationalisation of London local government, reported in 1960 and recommended amalgamating old metropolitan boroughs within the LCC area into bigger units, and forming other boroughs from the former districts of the Home Counties. These new boroughs were to be the primary housing authorities, although the Greater London Council was to have some supplementary role. Boroughs would also be responsible for personal and environmental health, welfare, libraries and roads other than main roads. The GLC was to control education and planning with 'statutory provision made in the administrative discharge of these responsibilities'. Among its other responsibilities were to be traffic, main roads, refuse disposal, fire and ambulance services, and an Intelligence Department which would 'collect, collate and disseminate information relevant to the performance of local government functions in Greater London'.

The Commission remarked in its report that the 'extraordinary complication of local government in Greater London is confusing to the electors and seems to induce in their minds a sort of fatalism, unless they can be whipped up by one or other of the political parties to vote on a national or quasi-national issue'. The aim of the reorganisation was to end this confusion by making the borough the primary unit of local government, with the GLC becoming involved only when the functions of government had to be performed over a wider area. The Commission said: 'The functions to be performed by each type of authority should be as far as possible self-contained without overlapping or duplication and without the necessity for delegation from one to another.' It added:

> We think it is of the first importance that the people of London should know who is responsible for what, and that the respective powers and functions should be so delimited that there is no need for delegation and other administrative contrivances, to which we have applied the phase 'papering over the crack'. Above all, we hope to get away from the conception of superior and inferior or upper and lower tier. We cannot emphasise too strongly that our proposed redistribution of functions is not on the basis of upper and lower, superior and inferior, but on the basis of wider and narrower.

It is clear that the people of London still do not know 'who is responsible for what', and still display the same electoral fatalism – perhaps because the results of the Commission's proposals were less self-contained and uncomplicated than they had hoped.

The London Government Act of 1963 incorporated Herbert's broad recommendations, with changes to create the Inner London Education Authority (ILEA) and fewer boroughs than Herbert proposed. London is now governed, in effect, by three bodies: the boroughs, the Greater London Council and central Government, principally through the Department of the Environment. The public also forms a part of the decision-making process. If, for example, a developer wishes to build a medium-sized office block, he must first get an Office Development Permit from the Department. This is then submitted to the borough council with a planning application. The application will then be sent to a number of local groups, and to some national societies if the scheme is in a conservation area or if historic buildings are involved. There may be protests from some or all of the groups. Even if the borough decides to give planning permission, the GLC may block the scheme, or the Department of the Environment may 'call it in' and order a public inquiry. The developer may get planning permission and think all is well, only to find that a building on the site previously thought of dubious merit is suddenly 'listed' for preservation and cannot be pulled down.

Building private houses may present similar problems. Tory outer boroughs, which grew up through the efforts of the speculative builders, may resist further development because they wish to maintain their open spaces and relatively quiet roads. Even where a borough agrees to a relatively low density scheme the GLC may use knowledge acquired under the Community Land Act to seek to acquire the land for council housing. Developers who have been refused permission can, of course, appeal to the Secretary of State for the Environment. But even if the appeal is successful, the developer may find that in the time that has elapsed the market has changed and his scheme is no longer viable.

The Department of the Environment generally sticks to its role of deciding global housing and transport budgets and acting as a court of appeal on planning issues. The GLC was always intended to deal with major strategic issues rather than the day-to-day matters which could be handled by the boroughs. But in practice, there is no clear division of responsibilities between the GLC and the boroughs. These overlapping powers can create tension between both kinds of local government and the confusion is compounded by the frequent changes of political control which ensure that the boroughs, the GLC and the Government are seldom ruled by the same political party for more than a few years at a time.

POLITICAL CONTROL OF CENTRAL AND LONDON GOVERNMENT

	Central government	**Greater London Council**	**London Boroughs Association**
1965	L	L	L
1966	L	L	L
1967	L	C	L
1968	L	C	C
1969	L	C	C
1970	C	C	C
1971	C	C	L
1972	C	C	L
1973	C	L	L
1974	L	L	L
1975	L	L	L
1976	L	L	L

Political control of constituencies in the GLC are[a] before the election in May 1977

Elected Labour MP in October, 1974

solid core Labour

1. Hackney Central
2. Hackney South & Shoreditch
3. Tower Hamlets, Bethnal Green & Bow
4. Tower Hamlets, Stepney & Poplar
5. Newham North-West
6. Newham South
7. Barking
8. Barking, Dagenham
9. Southwark, Bermondsey
10. Southwark ,Peckham

very safe Labour

11. Camden, St. Pancras North
12. Islington Central
13. Islington South & Finsbury
14. Haringey, Tottenham
15. Hackney N. & Stoke Newington
16. Waltham Forest, Walthamstow
17. Newham North-East
18. Wandsworth, Battersea North
19. Lambeth, Vauxhall
20. Lambeth Central
21. Lewisham, Deptford
22. Greenwich, Woolwich East

normally safe Labour

23. Hillingdon, Hayes & Harlington
24. Ealing, Southall
25. Hounslow, Feltham & Heston
26. Brent South
27. Brent East
28. Hammersmith North
29. Enfield, Edmonton
30. Haringey, Wood Green
31. Islington North
32. Camden, Holborn & St. Pancras South
33. Waltham Forest, Leyton
34. Havering, Hornchurch
35. Bexley, Erith & Crayford
36. Greenwich
37. Lewisham East
38. Southwark, Dulwich
39. Wandsworth, Tooting

Labour: key marginal

40. Enfield North ✱
41. Ealing North
42. City of Westminster, Paddington
43. Hammersmith, Fulham
44. Wandsworth, Putney
45. Wandsworth, Battersea South
46. Merton, Mitcham & Morden
47. Lambeth, Norwood
48. Lewisham West
49. Greenwich, Woolwich West
50. Redbridge, Ilford North
51. Redbridge, Ilford South

Elected Conservative MP in October, 1974

52. Hillingdon, Uxbridge
53. Hillingdon, Ruislip-Northwood
54. Harrow West
55. Harrow East
56. Harrow Central
57. Brent North
58. Barnet, Hendon North ■
59. Barnet, Chipping Barnet
60. Barnet, Finchley
61. Barnet, Hendon South
62. Enfield, Southgate
63. Haringey, Hornsey
64. Waltham Forest, Chingford
65. Redbridge, Wanstead & Woodford
66. Havering, Romford
67. Havering, Upminster
68. Camden, Hampstead ■
69. City of Westminster, St. Marylebone
70. Kensington & Chelsea, Kensington
71. Kensington & Chelsea, Chelsea
72. City of London & Westminster South
73. Ealing, Acton
74. Hounslow, Brentford & Isleworth ■
75. Richmond upon Thames, Twickenham
76. Richmond upon Thames, Richmond ❂
77. Kingston upon Thames
78. Kingston upon Thames, Surbiton
79. Merton, Wimbledon
80. Lambeth, Streatham
81. Sutton & Cheam ❂
82. Sutton, Carshalton ■
83. Croydon North-West ■
84. Croydon North-East ■
85. Croydon Central ■
86. Croydon South

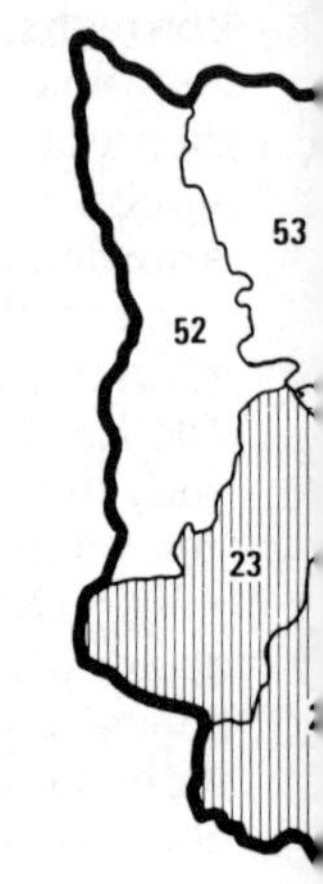

Most criticism has been levelled at the GLC. Journalists and ratepayers have found it difficult to understand quite what 32,000 people are doing at County Hall when many of their functions seem to be duplicated at borough level. Officers, councillors and politicians themselves have also voiced their unrest. Two small examples illustrate the point. In 1976 Derrick Blackhurst, a highly paid perma-

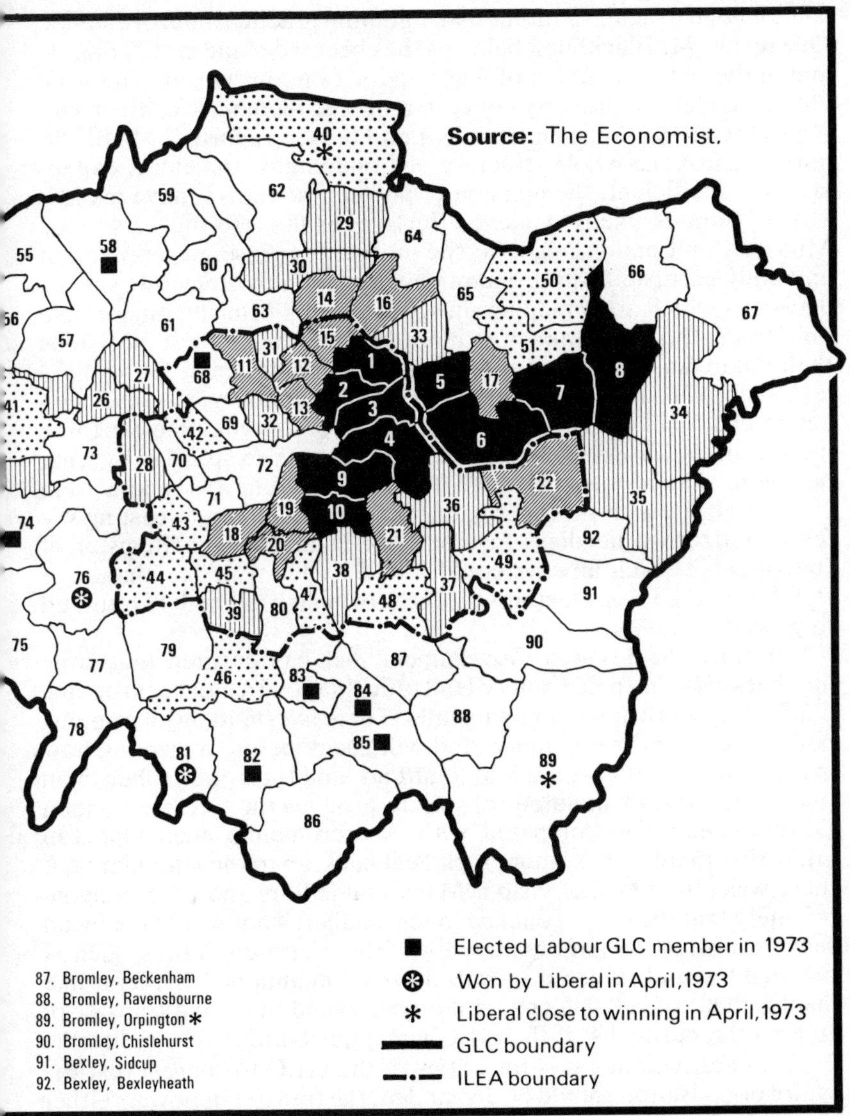

nent officer at assistant director-general level, retired early saying that since 1970 the GLC had changed considerably, and for the worse. The GLC staff magazine's editor, Len Hudson, reported Mr Blackhurst's view that whereas once, members of the Council had given first consideration to the need to achieve something worthwhile for London, now they tend to play to the gallery, promising what they cannot hope to achieve rather than initiating practical improvements. One result, Mr Blackhurst believes, has been a decline in staff morale and in the old satisfaction of working for London. He attributes the change largely to growing concern amongst members for their vulnerability at elections. Indeed, as Len Hudson reported, Mr Blackhurst regards the whole structure of London government as expensive and inefficient; the division of powers, he thinks, have made it virtually impossible to achieve effective results. He suggests that a Minister for London might be the answer, because, accepting that any body entrusted with London government must sometimes make decisions which are unpopular in some areas, a Minister answerable only to central Government is more likely to make those decisions than politicians, fearful of offending their constituents.

Also in 1976, a Labour alderman, Oliver Stutchbury, who had been acting chairman of the Policy and Resources Committee for three months in the absence of Illtyd Harrington, was so appalled by what he found that he resigned both from the Labour Party and from County Hall which he described as a 'gigantic charade costing my fellow citizens a needless fortune'. He established a 'Register of Individuals' which anyone could join for £10, with the chance of standing in the GLC elections pledged to abolish the body if returned to power.

Certainly the London Government Act has ensured that large numbers of highly paid County Hall officers spend a great deal of time duplicating work done in Town Halls. There is a standing joke among borough officers that County Hall will check before a meeting how many borough officers are due to attend, and then outnumber them two to one. It took hundreds of staff to produce the Greater London Development Plan compared with Abercrombie's nine. One can argue that there was far more technical back-up to the later plan; but there was also a lack of vision. Many councillors and officers agree privately that the GLC could be much smaller. That would not mean sacking most of the staff. Quite a few of the operations it runs, such as fire fighting and refuse disposal, must be maintained. Others, like management of 220,000 council homes, would involve a transfer of staff to the boroughs, if the GLC's responsibilities were reduced.

However tempting it is for critics of the GLC to suggest that the entire organisation should be disbanded, the transfer of powers either to the boroughs or to a Government Minister would raise more problems that the abolition of the GLC would solve. Boroughs would not agree among themselves on housing and transport issues: their inability to establish a common housing waiting list, road plans or traffic controls points to the need for a higher authority. If that authority were a Government Minister, London would be in danger of losing far more than it would gain. The Minister would himself have to defer to senior colleagues in housing, transport and other spending departments. There is no guarantee that London would do better than it does now, since other regions are already jealous of the metropolis and fight to reduce London's share. Londoners would gain a leader without real powers, but lose the right to vote him out of office at local elections if they disagreed with his decisions.

If the GLC is retained it should have fewer staff, but they should concentrate on key policy issues at a strategic rather than local level, unencumbered by the need to manage 220,000 council houses and scrutinise even minor planning applications for development. The boroughs already manage their own council houses and take a first look at planning matters; they could quite easily absorb the GLC's work and so avoid unnecessary duplication.

Another more radical suggestion is worthy of consideration. One of the main themes of this book is that London is spreading far beyond the boundaries of the GLC which were established in 1965, and that a ring city is developing out as far as the New Towns. The old London and the new ring are inextricably linked: the firms which have moved out to form the economic basis of the ring have strong business ties with London, and commuters travel from their homes in the ring into central London. Many other commuters drive back across the GLC boundary to work in centres like Croydon, Sutton and Kingston. Successive official housing reports have suggested that the problems of inner London will only be solved if more council homes are built around the edge of London, or inner London families are given access to those there already.

All this points to the need for an extension of the GLC boundaries *outwards* to encompass at least some of this buoyant ring. Perhaps an appropriate boundary would be just beyond the M25 ring by-pass now being constructed. The extension of the GLC boundary would serve at least two functions. First, it would help end the present rather fruitless argument about London's falling population. Instead of worrying about the precise number of people and firms still within the arbitrary boundary of the GLC, planners and politicians might concentrate more than they do upon who is moving and why. Secondly, a wider boundary would end the division of powers in housing, transport and planning which lead to so many problems. The problems would not disappear: the creation of the GLC has not ended the hostility between inner and outer London. But there might be some prospect in the longer term that the prosperity of the outer ring could be used to regenerate the inner city.

One proviso should be added to this suggestion. Under the reorganisation, the GLC would have to surrender its tenure of County Hall, where the spirits of the old London County Council continue to assure staff and members that they are really just like a big town council, forever anxious to see each traffic light in proper order. An enforced move would be made to new offices, housing only one-tenth of the staff. The rest would be transferred to the boroughs or other public bodies. No further offices would be allowed, and a strict control would be kept on the amount of paper in circulation. (Merit points would be awarded for the shortest committee reports, briefest research papers, with appropriate awards for star performers!)

The GLC's Director general, Sir James Swaffield, recently wrote of County Hall in the Local Government Chronicle:

> It should, above all, improve its public relations, not in the sense of bringing it closer to people, but in terms of conveying the importance of such an authority, its value for the future of London as a totality and for the future of local government over the whole of England. The attitude nowadays, which is reflected in an amendment of the old adage, "Those that can – do, those that can't – become bureaucrats", does a disservice not only to the individuals concerned, but to the whole of the government of the country.

The task of the new GLC administration must be to demonstrate this potential importance with action not words.

Suggested reading

The Plans: (all likely to be obtainable from reference libraries)
County of London Plan, 1943 by Abercrombie and Forshaw
Greater London Plan, 1944 by Abercrombie
Administrative County of London Plan, 1951: Statement and Analysis (see Analysis; Statement largely consists of zoning information) (London County Council)
First Review of ACLP, 1960 (London County Council)
Greater London Development Plan, Report of Studies and Statement, 1969 (GLC) The Report of Studies is informative in itself; the statement is instructive in showing how vague the Plan was.
Layfield Report (GLDP) Report of Committee of Inquiry 1973 2 vols; Vol 2 contains appendices only.
Statements by Department of the Environment: Conservatives, 1973, accompanying the Layfield Report; Labour, October 1975.
Modified GLDP August 1976
Strategy for the South East: 1976 Review, (Department of the Environment 1976)

Urban Planning:
The Exploding Cities, Peter Wilsher and Rosemary Righter (Andre Deutsch 1975) Based on an international conference.
Urban and Regional Planning, Peter Hall (Penguin 1974)
The Containment of Urban England, main author Peter Hall (for PEP by Allen and Unwin, 1973)

London Planning:
Planning for London, edited by Judy Hillman (Penguin 1971)
Urban Patterns, Problems and Policies edited by David Donnison, David Eversley

and others (Heinemann 1973); contains papers given to CES Seminar in 1972
Politics and Land Use Planning – The London Experience, Stephen Elkin (Cambridge University Press 1974)
A Guide to the Structure of London, Maurice Ash (Adams and Dart 1972)
London 2000 Peter Hall (see 1969 edition, Faber and Faber)
Governing the London Region, Donald L. Foley (University of California Press 1972)
Report of (Herbert) Commission on Local Government in Greater London (HMSO 1960)
The New Government of London, edited by Gerald Rhodes (Weidenfeld and Nicolson) Covering the aftermath of reform, 1965-1970
Too Much Government, Oliver Stutchbury (Baywell Press 1977)

EARNING A LIVING

Great Britain in 1977 is in the grip of the worst economic depression since the 1930s, with no prospect of a speedy recovery. Unemployment nationally is approaching 1.5 million and there are forecasts that it will rise inexorably to two million. Areas such as Liverpool have been worst hit, but in parts of south and east London more than one man in ten is without a job. In districts like Brixton, half of the young West Indians may be out of work. Between 1961 and the mid-1970s, the number of jobs available in the capital fell from 4.39 million to 3.99 million. The decline in industry has been seven times the national rate, while office work is expanding only half as fast as in the rest of the country. In central London new office blocks give a deceptive air of prosperity, for the number of office jobs is actually falling as firms save rents by relocating their clerical workers in the suburbs. Their places are taken by spacious board rooms and executive suites. There is a demand for top quality accommodation, but fewer workers are required.

London's buoyancy is being undermined by two factors. The first is inextricably bound up with national and international fortunes. When the country catches a cold London feels the chill, although not as badly as other regions. In that sense London's future, as much as any other city's, depends on the success of pay policy negotiations and national plans for economic revival. The Confederation of British Industry (CBI) has estimated, for example, that an increase in Britain's share of world exports of manufactured goods of just one per cent, plus the replacement of five per cent of our manufactured imports with home products, could generate another 550,000 jobs throughout the country. Without a national economic recovery of this kind, the best intentions of the GLC and Boroughs are bound to be frustrated. The second factor which has led to London's present depression is the cumulative effect of decisions made by successive sets of politicians and planners.

(RESIDENT) MALE UNEMPLOYMENT RATES (1971-1976)

	1971		1972		1973		1974		1975		1976	
	Apr	Oct	Apr	Oct	Apr	Oct	Apr	Oct	Apr	Oct	Apr	Oct
Great Britain	3.7	4.1	4.7	3.9	3.5	2.6	3.7	3.2	4.6	5.5	6.1	6.2
Greater London	2.7	2.8	3.2	2.8	2.5	1.8	2.3	2.2	3.3	4.3	5.4	5.5
Rest of South-East	2.4	2.4	2.7	2.1	1.9	1.5	1.9	1.9	2.9	3.5	4.1	4.1
Inner London	3.6	3.6	4.3	3.7	3.3	2.4	3.0	3.0	4.4	5.7	7.1	7.2

Source: based on Department of Employment statistics of the unemployed and on GLC estimates of the resident labour force in each area.

The last time that London's economy took a turn for the better was during the early 1970s. Nationally, unemployment in 1970 was running at about 500,000, inflation was 5.9 per cent and a Conservative Government was working on a possible economic growth forecast of four to five per cent a year. Now inflation is sixteen per cent and any growth is uncertain. In retrospect, it is easy to regret that instead of nurturing expansion there was an over-reaction against the very things that might have shored up London against the stormy weather ahead. Office buildings, roads, hotels and other facilities for tourists, all were seen merely as threats to London's heritage. Preservation of historic buildings, the evils of property development, tourism and motorway buildings were all packaged together by the conservation brigade into an area of concern which could be explored by journalists, myself included, without reference to boring and complicated economic arguments. New hotels were attacked because they sometimes involved demolition of homes and historic buildings, made money for developers and encouraged inconvenient tourists who jammed the pavements and asked the way on the tube. The plans to build a system of motorways to provide for rising car ownership among the middle-income groups provided those same people with splendid opportunities to organise coffee mornings and vilify councillors at protest meetings in the Town Hall. The sight of the GLC Conservative politician in charge of roads, Robert Vigars, staunchly enduring the verbal tomatoes, was one of the crueller delights of the time.

Contemporary books on London were about physical change rather than the social and economic forces that produced it. Christopher Booker and Candida Lycett Green's *Goodbye London* was not about the possible decline of a capital city, but the likely demolition of some hundreds of buildings of mixed architectural and historic interest. There was little thought of the extra jobs provided by hotels or of the tourists who were keeping alive the West End theatres, restaurants and shops. Offices were seen not as work places but as vehicles for speculation. Change, not economic stagnation, was considered the threat to London's future. Londoners were invited to consider, in effect, whether civilised life could possibly continue if the Coutts Bank 'pepperpot' building in the Strand was demolished, Charing Cross Road widened, Piccadilly Circus rebuilt, and Covent Garden turned into anything other than a cosy village for those people and firms currently enjoying cheap rents. The great sport was to stop things happening.

With Peter Walker anxious to make his name as the first Environment Secretary, and successors keen to keep the limelight, there was a strong sense among journalists that a few well displayed stories would prompt the Department of the Environment to 'call-in' a major office development for public enquiry, producing enough delay to kill the scheme, or spot-list a historic building to scupper a project which already had planning permission. Ministers could not resist the temptation to survey London from the eighteenth floor of their own unattractive office block in Marsham Street with a view to preventing anyone else building something better. Who cared if delay meant that a development company lost millions, or a change of heart would involve taxpayers and ratepayers in enormous compensation? Loud were the demands that the new Queen Anne's Mansions building designed by Sir Basil Spence on the edge of St James's Park should be reduced in bulk by about a third, even though Westminster Council would have had to pay Land Securities compensation estimated at £15 million. Now the building is up, it is difficult to remember what all the fuss was about.

Of course, many developers were totally insensitive in what they sought to demolish and in the quality of replacements. But few commentators balanced the destruction of older property against the introduction of greatly improved working conditions which the new office blocks might provide. There was every reason to be concerned about the environment, but instead of insisting that new schemes should be done well, conservationists often protested they should not be done at all.

The faltering economy

The mini-boom now looks like the final spurt of a flagging runner. London was not actually prospering in the way that the media and the politicians believed. The froth of activity was deceptive. Certainly the South East was the wealthiest area of the United Kingdom, but in 1970 it ranked only seventeenth out of forty-nine European regions. If during that final spurt motorways and more homes for sale had been available, the industrial jobs and skilled workers might not have left so fast. If office building had not been curbed at the centre, there might not now be unemployment among clerical staff. That brief respite in the early 1970s was the last chance for London to slow its decline. The politicians missed it.

EMPLOYMENT IN GREATER LONDON DIVIDED INTO THREE BROAD GROUPS

	Manufacturing industries	'Growth'* services	Other industries and services
1961	100	100	100
1962	98	103	103
1963	96	107	102
1964	94	108	102
1965	94	109	101
1966	91	114	101
1967	88	116	97
1968	84	118	96
1969	83	117	95
1970	79	120	89
1971	77	120	88
1972	71	123	88
1973	67	126	88
1974	66	128	86
1975	61	130	86

Index Series (1961 = 100)

*'Growth' Services comprised Insurance, Banking, Finance, Business Services, Professional and Scientific Services, Public Administration, Air Transport, Postal Services and Telecommunications, Miscellaneous Transport Services and Storage.

Sources: 1961, 1966, 1971 Census of Population (corrected). Other years: Department of Employment data adjusted to Census of Population equivalent.

OFFICE WORKERS IN CENTRAL LONDON

	1961	1966	1971	%change 1961-71
Professional & Managerial	220	239	264	+20%
Clerical	534	518	468	– 12.4%
Total	754	757	732	– 2.9%

All figures to nearest thousand.

Source: based on census data.

During their six years' control of County Hall, from 1967 to 1973, London Conservatives did make some attempts to reinforce London's role as a world city and capital. They took over Labour's motorway plans, proposed major redevelopment of Covent Garden and supported plans for a new exhibition centre. But under fierce attack from the conservationists they backed down and modified their plans.

For the GLC election of 1973, Labour showed concern for just the industrial sector of the economy while blaming growth in offices and tourism for social and environmental ills. The motorways which Labour had planned in 1965 were to be scrapped, industry encouraged, but all other areas of growth curtailed. GLC Labour leader, Sir Reg Goodwin, said at the time: 'Tory planning policy is to let the centre of London choke as more and more people come in to work in the ever growing office complex. Huge office blocks, like the infamous Centre Point, have stayed unlet. Yet in the surrounding streets people live in overcrowded slums.' It sounded good, although it was largely rubbish. The number of office jobs was falling, traffic speeds were rising and what Harry Hyams had to do with housing was never established. Labour won the election, though more, one suspects, because of Mr Heath's unpopularity than Sir Reg's charisma.

The underlying theme of Labour's policy document *London: the Future and You,* issued soon after Labour took control, was that London was a divided city and the major effort should be towards a redistribution of benefits. The accompanying press release said:

> Excessive growth of office employment concentrates an undue proportion of ability into commerce at the expense of the industrial sector; leads to an imbalance between the range of skills required and the range available in a socially balanced labour force; uses land which would otherwise be available for housing; and by overconcentrating jobs in the central area, creates pressure on the road system and public transport.
>
> Tourism, too, has added to the problems, for low wage rates paid to predominantly foreign workers have intensified the inner urban housing crisis. Additionally, new hotels have added to the strain on the transport system and other public services. It is for these reasons that the GLC will be asking the Government to consent to levying a tourist tax.

Where office development was to be allowed, Labour argued, it should be in the suburbs, near the homes of the workers, rather than in the centre, where major firms wanted at least some accommodation. Blandly, the paper said:

> In some areas there may be a temptation to permit developments which do not comply with this strategy, in order to increase the rate base. Although this is understandable, it would defeat the strategy. Should lack of local authority finance prove to be an obstacle to the implementation of the strategy, either alternative sources of local authority finance must be found, or the criteria for providing the grants by which Government returns to London some of the great wealth that it creates must be changed. The future of London is too important to be jeopardised by arbitrary financial conventions.

Over the next three years the Labour GLC and some Labour boroughs ruthlessly fought developments in the centre which promised to be successful in the belief that if plans for offices and hotels were turned down, then by some magic factories would spring up in their place. No matter if the developers promised to build homes as well, and provide a relatively wide range of jobs; they were seen purely as speculators and asset strippers to be resisted at all costs. The World Trade Centre at St Katharine's Docks was held up, a tough battle fought over the development of the old Gamages store site at Holborn Circus, and permission refused for Lyons to redevelop their Cadby Hall premises in Hammersmith. Wandsworth refused permission for development of the Morgan Crucible site on the Battersea waterfront, and even when Southwark's Labour council tried to reach agreement with the developers of Hays Wharf on the south bank opposite the City, the GLC resisted. In areas of major development like Covent Garden and Docklands, the emphasis was to be on providing whatever the locals wanted, whether or not it had any relevance to London's strategic needs. The GLC's leaders, while forever protesting that they had a budget in the top forty of national league tables and so deserved at least the status of regional government, displayed all the vision of a parish council.

While curbing growth in those operations which work well in a capital – offices and tourism – the Labour GLC harried the Government for changes to assist flagging industry. They urged the abolition of the Industrial Development Certificate (IDC) system, under which firms have to get special permission for new factories or major expansion in London; and to jog what they saw as Government complacency, they announced at the end of 1975 that they were considering ending co-operation in the 'export' of firms and people to the New Towns, and other Expanding Towns with which they had agreements. In fact the IDC restrictions and the New Town agreements have been demonstrated to have relatively minor effects on London industry. By the 1970s the decline was due more to factors like the lack of sites for expansion, poor roads and a lack of skilled workers. In concentrating its attack on controls, Labour was in effect flogging a dead horse; the inexorable movement of industry out of London had begun as long ago as the 1930s and was only spurred on by Abercrombie's plan.

Dispersing industry

At that time, the Government was desperately seeking measures with which to tackle the massive unemployment in areas dominated by basic industries like mining, engineering and textiles. A fall in world demand for Britain's basic exports had left areas of the north stranded with no growth points, while the new industries of electrical engineering, motor vehicles, aircraft and pharmaceuticals were expanding in the Midlands and around London. The Barlow Commission, set up to consider the problem, recommended in 1940 controls on further expansion in Greater London and Patrick Abercrombie, one of the Commission's members, incorporated the proposals in the official plans for London that he presented to the Government in 1943 and 1944. Abercrombie recognised that industry was already moving out of central London to the edges in search of better sites for expansion, and he proposed to reinforce this movement.

Not only was industry discouraged from starting or growing in London, the planners were anxious to uproot some of the 'non-conforming' industry that was already there and replace it with housing as part of comprehensive development schemes. The County of London Plan said of the East End and some of the south London boroughs:

> Here an industrial survey has revealed a veritable peppering of whole districts with factories, many of them of very small size, which have insinuated themselves into real residential areas, producing a hybrid type of development. There is much that is popular and convenient about this mixture of work-places and homes, where indeed in many cases the factories are actually in the homes themselves. Any regrouping of industry must take this characteristic of so much of London's work into consideration. But it may be generally stated that economical site planning for factories must satisfy very different requirements from that for houses. In the areas which need almost total rebuilding it will not be difficult to remedy this defect and at the same time to preserve the advantages of people living near their work and of the small-scale type of industry in which London has always specialised.

In the event, the new factories built during redevelopment were too costly and many firms did not survive the transplant. They died.

In 1943 the Thames was still central to London's economy. The County of London Plan reported:

> In many ways the docks and riverside industrial areas can be described as the primary source of London's commercial life. They form the main shipping, distribution and manufacturing centre on which depends the business of the City, the distributive trades of the West End and the livelihood of so many of London's inhabitants. In location the sources of work follow a logical arrangement – the docks served by the Thames to the east and distributing to the adjacent industries; the City, immediately to the west, centre of business and intermediary between production and distribution; and the West End, main centre of retail distribution.

Abercrombie had expected the docks to remain active for the foreseeable future. Indeed, his strategy depended upon the continuing vitality of the Port of London, and the continuing establishment of new industry on purpose-built estates away from housing. But by the 1960s plans to shift working downstream to Tilbury, increased containerisation and the decline of dock trade as Britain lost cargoes previously guaranteed by the Empire, had cut employment dramatically; the London Docks labour force, for instance, fell from 31,000 in 1955 to 9,800 in 1975. Too often, firms uprooted by redevelopment had found new premises too expensive.

Since 1961 London has lost a further half-million manufacturing jobs – a drop of thirty-four per cent compared to a five per cent drop in the rest of the country. At the same time there has been a twenty-one per cent increase in the rest of the South East, showing not just that firms had moved out of London, but that the capital was no longer such a good place in which to start up industry. The biggest cause of decline was the closure of firms or their shedding of workers. Less than twenty per cent had gone to the assisted areas or New Towns as Abercrombie had wished.

At the same time as London was losing industrial jobs in the 1950s, so it was gaining office jobs, particularly in insurance, finance, banking and business services like accountancy, law and management consultancy. City institutions such as Lloyds, the Baltic Exchange, the Stock Exchange, banking and commodity markets grew from Britain's dominant world trade situation. Their success has been to survive Britain's decline as a trading nation, capitalise on their expertise and become world leaders in financial services.

Curbing offices

Until the early 1960s, office jobs in the centre continued to grow against the tide of falling employment there. But by midway through the decade even offices joined the outward ebb. The Government was not to know this until the 1966 census results were published, and in 1965, in the mistaken belief that office jobs were still growing, they adopted similar tactics to those used against industry in the 1950s. Developers were required to have office development permits (ODPs) from the Government before they could even apply to councils for planning permission to put up office blocks, and the Location of Offices Bureau (LOB) was set up to encourage firms to leave London for less fortunate regions. After the controls were imposed, the 1966 census showed that the total workforce in the centre had dropped 4.6 per cent since 1961. There were more office blocks, certainly, but already office workers who had previously been cramped together were getting more space in the new buildings. In the next five years total employment in central London fell by 6.4 per cent, office employment by 3.3 per cent.

The Labour GLC administration elected in 1973 perpetuated the Government's mistake. Councillors were convinced that all those office blocks going up must mean increasing congestion, and they set their officers to work to prove it. The GLC office policy, produced in Spring 1975, anticipated an expanding Greater London economy where office jobs would increase from 1.535 million in 1966 to an estimated 1.702 million in 1981. The GLC reckoned that there would be about 60,000 jobs and the prospects of nowhere for the office employees to work. Since the GLC did not want these extra jobs to be in central London, the new policy called for all new office building to be concentrated in the suburbs except for three million square feet which would be allowed in central London to meet special cases, including developments over railway stations. All boroughs were given special allocations of floorspace.

In the middle of 1976 it began to dawn on the Government and the GLC politicians that curbs on office development in central London could have done untold damage. The LOB had, in twelve years' existence, assisted over 121,000 jobs to move from central London, and perhaps the same number again had moved of their own accord. But only ten per cent of these had gone to areas of high unemployment; most simply went to other areas in the South East. The parallel with industry was unmistakeable. The Government's Office Location Review reported that it expected firms to continue to move from the centre to escape high rents, rates and wage costs, but also suggested that once the economy picked up and firms began to expand there would be more demand for office space in the centre. So the frequently advanced arguments that the centre had enough offices already did not hold good. On the other hand, all the fears advanced in the mid 1960s about extra congestion caused by offices were unfounded, the Review concluded. It recommended the abolition of the ODP system, and a change in role for the LOB.

The point was taken in County Hall. A GLC report commenting on the Review said:

> It is important not to overlook the possibility and danger of a decline in office employment in London which would be compounded with the heavy decline in manufacturing employment. Office jobs have been forming an increasing proportion of London's total employment, in part helping to make up some of the manufacturing jobs that London has lost.

This downward trend could now be made worse by several other factors: cuts in public spending could mean fewer jobs for civil servants and council workers (the Government is also planning to export 30,000 civil servants to the regions); major banks and insurance companies are moving staff out of London; and on top of that, further moves towards automation, new techniques and improved telecommunications, could all mean fewer jobs for office workers. Property correspondents and estate agents have warned that London could lose international companies because of a shortage of appropriate office space. Frankfurt, Paris and Brussels offer fully air conditioned office buildings with large floor areas at lower rents and are challenging the world-supremacy of London's telecommunications system. Foreign companies demand high standard accommodation which simply is not available in London. Bruce Kinloch wrote in the *Daily Telegraph* in August 1976:

> If the City of London is to retain its hold on international trade and continue its high contribution to Britain's invisible exports, ways must be found, and found quickly, to provide offices which are suitable to overseas companies. Over half of the remaining three million square feet of offices available in the City consists of property which was built prior to 1950 or built or modernised since 1950 without air conditioning. There is only just over 500,000 square feet of office built or modernised since 1950 with air conditioning inside the central area.

In the new atmosphere of concern the GLC has recently agreed to large office development over Liverpool Street Station, for the Baltic Exchange and Chase Manhattan bank, all in the City. But controls may have been relaxed too late. The Community Land Act, the Development Land Tax and other measures have killed confidence that property companies could clamber out of disastrous situations such as the one they found themselves in after the collapse of 1974. In 1977, many companies are being kept afloat by the banks who fear foreclosure on debts. Most property companies are prepared to risk little more than collect the rents on the property they – or rather their banks – own.

In view of the present trend for offices to disperse to the suburbs, one might suggest that planners abandon any overall office location policy, and simply make sure the buildings are attractive and conveniently located. Similarly one might argue that since industry has such an uphill struggle in London, it is fruitless to try and re-establish manufacturing there. However, new offices and factories do make substantial differences to an area. Shops and cafes spring up because they can sell newspapers and cigarettes, sandwiches, haircuts and groceries to the office workers as well as local residents. If some areas are particularly lacking in these amenities, while others are well endowed, it is reasonable to nudge the offices to areas in most economic need of them. The difficulties arise when planners are too rigid in enforcing their policies. Developers are confronted with take-it-or-leave-it situations in which they feel they have no choice. The result may be that expansion is prevented in areas which the developers favour, while areas designated by the planners remain barren. Roger Hardman reported in the *Estates Times* of November 1976 that the GLC policy of encouraging office development in the preferred locations has had minimal effect: 'Areas like Croydon and Sutton, which were in great demand before the [GLC policy] came into being, continue to have more demand for space than they can handle, with ODPs and GLC opposition being the chief restraining factors.' Whereas, to quote but two examples of "preferred locations": 'Woolwich has not noticed any upsurge in demand [and] . . . Walthamstow has to date been . . . a non-starter.'

Political prescriptions

The problem for industry is rather different, since there is less evident demand for starting up factories in London. Restrictions and the greater profitability of office development in the past have deterred developers from embarking on industrial schemes. There is a case for councils not only making life as easy as possible for any firm which wishes to expand premises, or any developer who wishes to build, but also to test the water by offering, for example, to help with site assembly. Planners are now ringing up developers asking them to build factories, instead of just refusing them permission to put up office blocks.

There is realisation on all sides, however, that regenerating industry in London or anywhere else is going to depend on more fundamental economic and political changes than easing up on IDCs or even council-built factories.

Broadly, three political prescriptions for regeneration are being canvassed at present. They might be described as Right, Left and central Labour.

The Tory, and Confederation of British Industry (CBI), line is that confidence in the private sector must be restored both nationally and locally. There should be less taxation, less intervention, higher profitability, and housing and transport policies that favour the skilled worker and enterprising firm. Tommy Macpherson, who is chairman of the London and South East Council of the CBI, said:

> London is an expensive place to work and manufacture in, just as New York is, because you pay the rates that support not just a town but a capital city. Therefore we must switch as fast as possible to a skilled and semi-skilled labour production which puts the greatest possible added value on the goods we are producing, and so gives the extra income. This will prove an

enormous and difficult change in London, because of the move away of skilled labour and because the vast proportion of unemployed in London are very unskilled indeed. Unskilled, male labour will, on the whole, go to space-demanding industries like warehousing which are too expensive to run in a capital city because of the rates bill. The type of industry you ought to have in London is, say, electronics – a small space consumer and a high skill operation. The first practical move should be to improve the climate for industry in London so much that the successful firms that already operate here will want to expand in London rather than move elsewhere. Then new entrants may want to start in London. After all there are great advantages – Britain's biggest market is at your doorstep. Unfortunately, it happens to be terribly difficult either to start in business or to keep going. There are so many regulations to comply with if you are starting up, and once under way your fixed costs are high – rents, rates and so on. If we in the CBI really believed there had been a total change of attitude by the GLC (who are considered, fairly or unfairly, to be hostile to industry and longing to get it out of the place and make London nice and tidy for civil servants), then people would breathe a sigh of relief and look to expand here.

As well as this new climate I think there has to be some moderation of the tremendously escalating rates bill borne by industry. Secondly, there should be a very much more determined attempt to improve the transport infrastructure. The slowness with which it has been developed in London is really terrifying when you look at other big cities. If you are going to encourage manufacturing or distributive industry, transport is a very high priority indeed. People in large businesses or in small must be able to bring their goods in, take their goods away again, and deliver their goods to the customer. There are a lot of customers in London.

Thirdly, there must be some endeavour to solve the housing problem for the supervisory and skilled labour level who on the whole do not want to be council house dwellers. The shortage of skilled labour is a very wide national problem, but in London it has been intensified by skilled labour moving out of the decaying areas of London because they could get housing in Harlow or Milton Keynes or somewhere like that, and also get highly paid skilled jobs there. Within London itself, it is impossible to get skilled labour in west London, but I'm told by my trade union colleagues that in north London there is a surplus. However, communication is so difficult that although they may be only ten miles apart, the labour won't transfer.

Fourthly, we need an end to the constant pin-pricks against the small benefits supervisory staff and general management feel it reasonable for them to have – principally pin-pricks on their owning and using a motor car in the city area.

Finally, we must solve the intense problem that London has the most difficult, bureaucratic, slow and comprehensive set of building restrictions that I've ever come across anywhere in the world.

As an international centre what is important for London is, first, what's going to happen to sterling balances, and, second, the GLC recognising that white-collar workers are desirable workers, that they have legitimate aspirations. Because if the GLC went and looked we could get into London a tremendous amount of Common Market business – institutional, commercial and industrial head or branch offices which are not coming because there are restrictions on offices and there's a bad atmosphere.

London has got to have a future; we can't afford to let it fall into the decay that is beginning. And it's not wholly going to be done by dramatic gestures like £1,200 million on the Docklands scheme. It's going to be done by a change in attitude, almost for the GLC to say, we are the businessman's Government, we want you, we love you, baby.

The Left line on industrial regeneration is closely identified nationally with Energy Secretary Tony Benn, and has found expression in reports by a number of Home Office-backed Community Development Projects (CDP). The analysis is that the problems of industry, and inner city decline, have their roots in the nature of capitalism. Capital moves to the area currently most profitable, abandoning in its wake the workers of the ports, textile mills and shipbuilding industries. Multi-national companies import and export capital as wage rates and other local conditions change. Government is relatively powerless against these forces, and attempts to shift industry from place to place by investment grants and controls have little effect. Judith Hart MP wrote in a foreword to a CDP report, *The Cost of Industrial Change,* in February 1977:

When power came from coal and steam, factories had to stay where they were. When Engels wrote of Manchester in 1844, and Charles Booth wrote of the condition of the working people of London later in the century, industry, with all its smoke and grime and its inhumanity, with all the poverty and squalor of the living conditions in the housing areas which surrounded it, was rooted where it was. But electricity changed all that: and it was the profound nature of that particular technological change which brought industrial location into the centre of twentieth-century interventionist planning.

Judith Hart identifies a second factor, more influential as a determinant in recent years.

> Depression has returned to haunt European capitalism and the profits of decline contribute to the familiar city centre fringe: It houses a succession of garages, maintenance depots, discount sales, vehicle distribution, used cars, parts merchants, carpet warehouses, night clubs, drive-in chip shops and storage firms. They require few workers and tend to pay them badly.
>
> The report suggests positive planning and intervention must take the place of the demonstrated failure of carrots-and-sticks strategies. It suggests that the nature of our urban crisis, and its consequences for the human condition, may perhaps only be capable of solution within a framework of radical economic policies. But while these conclusions are debatable – and will be challenged – they derive from an impeccable historical analysis, which must be studied (I hope it will) by Peter Shore and his officials in the Department of the Environment. Their study ought to lead them to the view that this is a debate whose remit cannot be contained within any narrow framework. It is about the whole direction our society is to take to meet the human need.

The report calls for public ownership of profitable industry as well as 'lame ducks', and a far wider role for the National Enterprise Board in the purchase of controlling holdings in firms, the enforcement of planning agreements between Government, unions and employers, and ensuring unions have the right to examine the forward strategies of large companies. It concludes:

> Until policies are implemented which seriously challenge the rights of industry and capital to move freely about the country (not to mention the world) without regard for the welfare of workers and existing communities – who end up carrying the costs under the present system – the problems and inequalities generated by uneven capitalist development will persist.

In October 1976 the Labour-controlled Wandsworth council produced a report which proposed implementing this alternative strategy locally. It called for local planning agreements with firms, encouragement of worker co-operatives, and more trading by the council itself. However the greatest care was to be taken in selecting which firms should be allowed to develop in the borough:

> While jobs are a paramount need, other principles are also important. Importing firms which pay sub-standard wages, impose sub-standard working conditions, or infringe the rights of

work people, would be unacceptable. And in seeking to attract jobs the council must guard against simply recreating the situation which gave rise to the present crisis, in which the crucial decisions on Wandsworth's economy have been taken by people and institutions remote from Wandsworth's problems.

It would be intolerable for public money to be used to create industrial assets simply so that these could be looted and pillaged by a new generation of asset strippers.

The answer to this dilemma must lie in greater democratic accountability in the distribution of funds to industry; an improved economic planning system, with a major role for local government; and experiments in new forms of industrial ownership and control.

Other Labour groups, including that at County Hall, waver between the more polarised Left and Right positions. The general line is that industrialists should be given permissions, loans and advice: some factories should be built; and Government should be asked to remove restrictions. The 1977 GLC Labour Manifesto said:

Two million pounds is being spent this year on building factories in Lambeth, Tower Hamlets and Hackney – already firms have moved in and jobs have been created. Plans are also in an advanced state for the acquisition of a site in Park Royal for modern workshops. A new Industrial Centre has been set up at County Hall, staffed with professionals to advise London industrialists on their problems and keep them in London. The next Labour GLC will expand its assistance to industry in both the field of economics and information. Work is already in hand to provide an industrial development package service for industry, based at County Hall, which would be able to meet all the needs of a potential industrialist wishing to set up in London from the offer of suitable sites, to planning permission advice and help over transport, labour and so on.

The next stage is the creation of an Industrial Development Agency for London, with its strategic policy controlled by the GLC but with operational freedom to attract major employers back to London and to nurture and promote industrial development.

Labour will continue to press the Government to lift its restrictions on industrial expansion in the London area. Already there has been some limited success in persuading Government to apply the same conditions on Dockland industry as in New Towns and raise the limit on factory size requiring Industrial Development Certificates.

The Left Alternative Strategy and the CBI approach both depend for their local success upon the establishment of different national economic strategies. The CBI approach relies upon there being fewer planning controls, lower taxation, and a Government which believes in encouraging profit. Each strategy has its own internal logic, and which you choose depends upon a preference for state control or private enterprise.

The Labour middle-of-the-road line falls between the two stools. It depends upon the regeneration of confidence among industrialists without explicitly offering the prospect of profitability which is essential for this. As a back-up, Labour councillors call for the National Enterprise Board to invest public money in London industry – a course of action hardly feasible unless a Left Government is in power and prepared to increase the NEB budget considerably.

There is a danger that London will get the worst of all possible worlds, that the tangle of controls will remain, confidence will not pick up, and neither private nor public finance will be forthcoming. Even if the new administration at County Hall, and boroughs and Government departments, were to promise not to hold back expansion by a tangle of regulations, they would be unable to keep their pledge. Once a council officer or civil servant is appointed to enforce a regulation it is unrealistic to expect him to stop on someone else's say so. Suppose a planning permission is challenged in law, or relaxation of a fire regulation leads to a fatal blaze? Whose head is on the block? Controls are far easier to impose than relax. One can appreciate the planners' concern that all controls should not be swept aside in panic-stricken anxiety to allow any development which promises a few jobs. Just as the concern for protecting the environment swung too far, so too can the jobs-at-any-price movement. We are still trying to clear up the results of Victorian laissez faire development of industry.

But while continuing to ensure that factories and offices are safe, well-located and properly designed, local authorities could take a fresh look at housing and transport policies which contribute to the success or failure of employment policies. Firms consistently stress that good transport and attractive housing prospects for skilled workers are major factors in determining whether they leave London or stay, expand or die. The next two chapters suggest that there is plenty for councils to do in putting their own houses in order, as well as worrying about what Whitehall and Westminster are up to.

Suggested reading

The City in the World Economy, William Clarke (The Institute of Economic Affairs 1965)

An Economic Study of the City of London, John Dunning and Victor Morgan (Allen and Unwin 1971)

The Office Location Review (Department of the Environment 1976)
Changing Structure of the Labour Force (Department of Employment 1975)
Industrial Movement and Regional Development – The British Case, Morgan Sant (Pergamon 1975)
Community Development Project publications including 'The Cost of Industrial Change' (CDP Editorial Team 1977) and *Aims of Industry* (Newham CDP 1974)
Strategy for the South East; 1976 Review, Economy report (Department of the Environment 1976)

MOVING AROUND THE CITY

The frustrations of commuting into London or just getting around town are going to increase over the next few years. Congestion will get worse as more people buy cars and try to use them on inadequate roads with surfaces showing more cracks and potholes. Bus, tube and rail fares are all likely to rise faster than wages or prices. Yet most services will not be improved, and buses may be cut by up to a third. If there is one bright spot, it is that the standard of tube services should be maintained, partly because the large numbers of tourists, who use the underground extensively, now provide twenty per cent of London Transport's total revenue. It is unlikely, though, that any more lines will be built after the opening of the Piccadilly Line extension to Heathrow, and the Fleet Line from Baker Street to the Strand. Hopes of a new tube from Chelsea to Hackney are unrealistic and a £200 million extension of the Fleet Line through east London to Thamesmead looks uncertain because of doubts about whether it offers the best value for money in regenerating Docklands. With nearly everyone caught in the grip of rising costs and falling services, the one group with cause to cheer will be the Japanese manufacturers of mopeds and motorcycles. Between 1975 and 1976, the number of two-wheelers on the road increased by over twenty per cent, as people braved the weather to save fares, avoid jams and find free parking.

The reason for this gloomy picture is simple: the Government has decided that what little money there is will go into industry and housing rather than transport. Consequently subsidies are being cut, so fares must increase road building and maintenance will be reduced, and there will be little money to improve public transport. With money so tight, and such little room for manoeuvre, certain decisions may seem obvious, if unpopular. Put up fares for long-distance commuters, because they tend to be better off. Curb car use in the city centre, because that helps buses get through the jams, and drivers can always transfer to public transport. Abandon all

Urban growth and the development of London's transport system

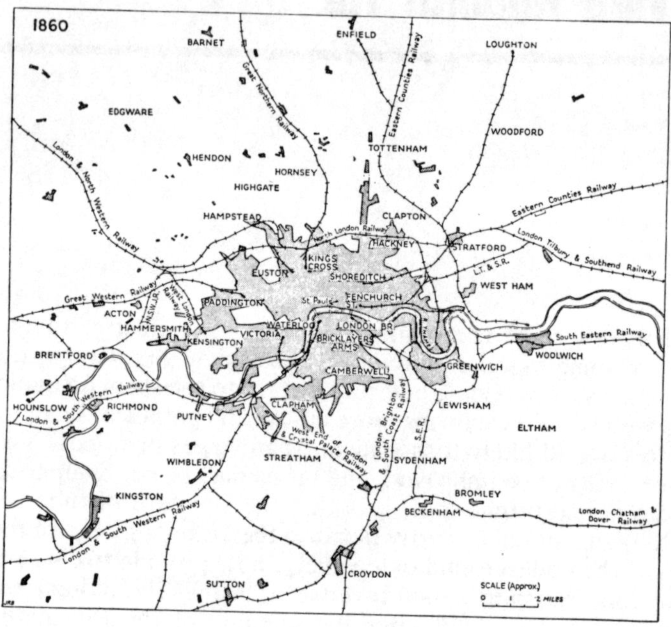

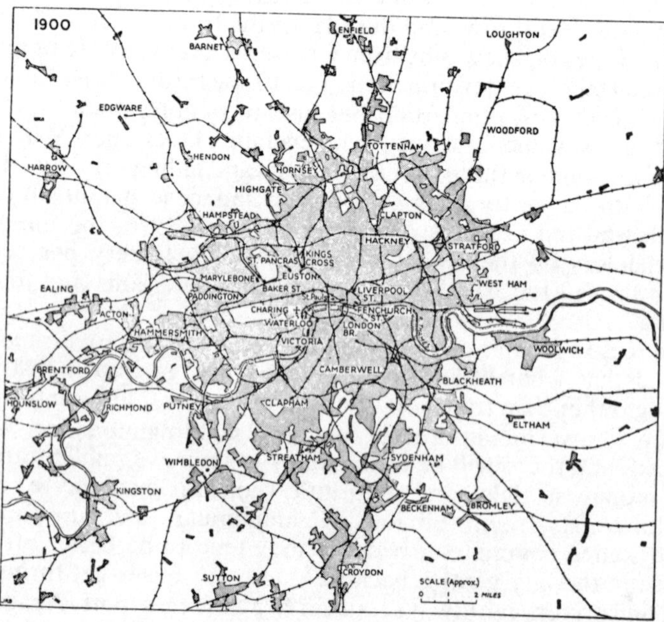

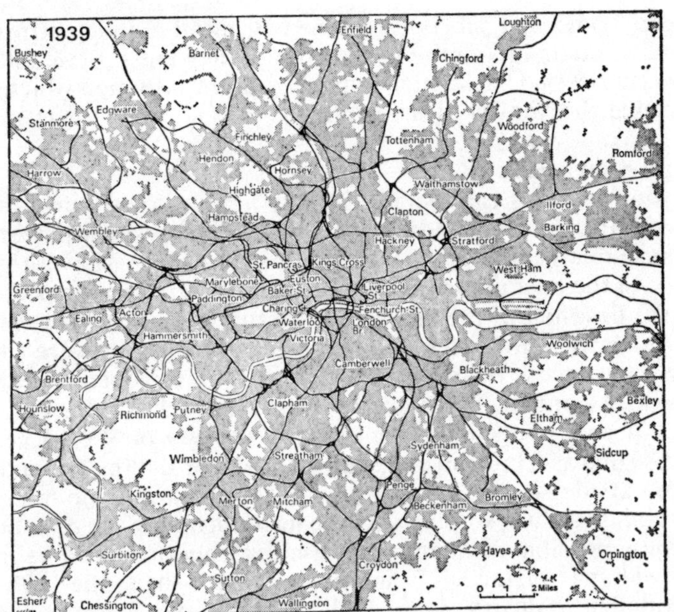

Source for all three maps: *A History of London Transport* by T. C. Barker and M. Robbins (Allen and Unwin/London Transport).

road building within London, and concentrate on one major ring road by-pass around the outskirts so that through traffic does not have to fight its way into the centre and out again. In the long term, encourage people to live nearer their work, and to walk to the shops and the pub so that they can keep fares down and save petrol.

Some of these policies may well be adopted, but each has a snag when put into practice. Cutting car use in the centre means tough parking controls on private spaces under office blocks, and a special licencing system to prevent through traffic taking up the road space vacated; both measures would be difficult to police, and might well damage businesses by preventing customers and staff reaching their premises. Giving buses greater priority would not improve services dramatically; studies have shown that mechanical faults and problems of control are as much to blame for unreliability as congestion. Putting up fares rapidly for long-distance commuters, and ending road building, each present more fundamental problems because London, like all cities, has developed as a result of its transport system; it has grown outwards as travel has become easier. People have carefully weighed up travel time and cost against house prices and amenities. If that balance is suddenly upset, the lifeline between home and job is threatened. Central London firms may suddenly find that to recruit and keep staff they must move out to the suburbs or beyond, so starting a spiral of decentralisation which could undermine the vitality of the centre.

The quest for space

Transport policies can dictate the way a city grows – or dies. The history of the last one hundred and fifty years shows how powerful an influence this is; the history of the last ten years shows that the lessons of the past are inevitably tempered by political expediency.

In the first half of the nineteenth century, suburban houses were the prerogative of the rich, whose secluded mansions were situated within easy access by private carriage of both the open countryside and central London. Fares on horse-drawn coaches were very high; in 1825 it cost two shillings to travel to the city or West End from suburbs such as Clapham or Peckham, and one shilling and sixpence for the outside seats. Clerks in the city were earning no more than thirty shillings a week. Only with the introduction of the omnibus did it become possible for many middle-class Londoners to live farther than walking distance from their work; then the suburban development industry flourished. In 1848 the *Morning Herald* remarked, 'the villa mania is everywhere most obtrusive'. Throughout the suburbs were 'eligible family residences, desirable villas and aristocratic cottages which have nothing in the world of the cottage about them except the name'. George Emerson reported that 'Kentish Town is throwing out lines of bricks and mortar to meet its neighbours, Hampstead Heath and Downshire Hill . . . Dalston has thrown out long lines of handsome villas across the fields and orchards . . . Clapton has developed itself on the north-east'. A contemporary guidebook drew attention to 'Herne Hill and Champion Hill, which are studded with gentlemen's seats, and from the elevations of which fine views are gained of the picturesque landscapes of Kent and Surrey'. Peckham Rye is described as 'a favourite resort for invalids . . . there is not in the immediate neighbourhood of London a more open and agreeable country than Peckham Rye, Nunhead, Forest Hill and the adjacent localities'.

In the second half of the century, national prosperity increased demand for commercial and business floorspace in the City, forcing rents up and squeezing out houses. London's rising population could only be accommodated by building outwards. Real earnings rose and, as transport fares fell, more and more people could afford to use public transport. The growth of the railway system, the introduction of workmen's tickets and the rapid extension of the tramways network in the 1870s enabled more and more people to live in the suburbs and work in the centre. The first workmen's trains in London were run by the Metropolitan Company. In 1864 it ran two such services, costing three pence return and starting respectively at 5.30 and 5.40 in the morning. The *Building News* did not exaggerate in saying that 'the invasion of the metropolis by the 'Steam Horse' has, during the last quarter of a century, produced changes not only in the physical features of the metropolis, but also in the manners, customs, mode of living, and even in the thoughts of its inhabitants, which are almost incredible. For a century previous to the year 1836, stagnation was the order of the day; but then came the locomotive into London, and all was changed.'

During the nineteenth century, London's population had increased six times to 6,580,000. In 1900 the *Building News* reported:

> There is a great flood . . . which has overtaken London and our great cities with houses and dwellings for the middle and working classes . . . Go where we will – north, south, east or west of this huge over-grown Metropolis – the fungus-like growth of houses manifests itself stretching from town to suburb and village – as from the southern suburbs to Herne Hill and Dulwich, and from Streatham to Croydon. In every direction we see the same outward growth of dwelling houses of a small and unpretending class – generally a repetition of a type of house that has been found to meet the requirements of the middle class and artisan. The larger and more commodious residence of fifty years ago is being pulled down, or swamped by this tide of small houses: where a large house existed, ten or a hundred or more have been built, absorbing the acres of gardens and private park lands. This is one of the social revolutions of the age.

Municipal authorities began to take advantage of cheap travel by building estates outside central London to reduce continuing problems of overcrowding. Twentieth-century policy followed that example – London continued to grow as it had in the nineteenth, and for similar reasons: greater economic activity, more employment and ever-increasing mobility. Introduction of the car was not, however, accompanied by expansion of the road system. The Royal Commission on London Traffic in 1905 heard considerable expert evidence urging the need for wide roads encircling London at a radius of twelve miles from Charing Cross. But such proposals had little impact upon the Commission.

Homes before roads

After the First World War some progress was made: the North Circular Road was constructed, as were the Kingston, Watford and Croydon by-passes, but many schemes remained uncompleted. Between 1900 and 1939 car ownership had risen from 2,000 to

330,000. Rapid growth in car ownership and the number of commuters produced mounting congestion in inner London. The 1943 County of London Plan stated that 'the most obvious and ubiquitous defect in pre-war London was that of traffic, both the congestion in the streets and the strap-hanging in tubes, suburban trains and buses', adding the dire warning that 'the need for improved traffic facilities in and around London has become so acute, that unless drastic measures are taken to relieve a large number of the thoroughfares, crossings and junctions of their present congestion, there will be grave danger that the whole traffic system will, before long, be slowed down to an intolerable degree'. Professor Patrick Abercrombie, principal author of the plan, envisaged that the post-war period would herald 'the age of mobility'. Seeing the need to plan ahead, he proposed major road building to improve travel to and from the centre and to allow through traffic to by-pass the built-up areas. The proposals were for five ring roads and ten radial roads. The ringway system was born. Yet money was scarce after the war and the now familiar cry of 'homes before roads' put paid to Abercrombie's plans. New roads would have meant the displacement of houses, businesses and industry making the proposals less environmentally and socially acceptable and more costly as time progressed.

The late 1940s and early 1950s saw the peak of public transport use in London. Thereafter it declined as car ownership rose. During the winter of 1958 Abercrombie's prediction became reality – central London literally seized up time and again. According to the Road Research Laboratory, the average speed of peak-hour traffic in central London fell to eight miles an hour in 1959 (compared with over fourteen miles per hour in 1976). In 1960, the London County Council stated that its transport budget, which allowed for an average level of expenditure of £6 million a year, 'gives no scope for an ambitious plan of new highways'. The London and Home Counties Traffic Advisory Committee warned that 'unless radical action is taken, traffic will come to a standstill in the (central) area within five years'. But it was not road building but traffic management which came to the rescue. By rationalising intersections and introducing strategically-placed roundabouts and parking controls and one-way streets total congestion was avoided.

It was generally agreed that the main cause of congestion was insufficient road space, but nothing was forthcoming from the Ministry of Transport. An emergency debate on London's traffic congestion came and went in October 1965 and, on the day of the debate, the *Evening Standard* commented that 'the Ministry of Transport awaits the report of a study group. The Ministry assures us that it is studying the problem. But London's traffic chaos has been the subject of continuous study for years. It is not an overnight revelation and it is about time that the Minister of Transport came up with some concrete suggestions.' The issue came to a head with the creation of the Greater London Council, whose controlling Labour Party, in its first press conference in April 1965, outlined yet another plan for constructing three ring roads to serve the London area. These proposals were later embodied in the 1969 Greater London Development Plan, which observed that 'the road system in Greater London . . . is probably less well endowed than any other major urban centre in Western Europe that has reached a similar stage of economic growth'.

The road proposals were vehemently opposed because they involved the demolition of about 30,000 homes in close-knit communities, and would cost at least £2,000 million. Frank Layfield's Committee of Inquiry in 1973 recommended that some of the roads should be built. The Conservative Environment Secretary, Geoffrey Rippon, agreed; but by then the leaders of the Labour GLC group had decided the major road proposals were a liability for the election of that year, and promised not to build any of them. When Socialist Environment Secretary, Anthony Crosland, replaced Mr. Rippon, the Labour GLC got him to agree that certainly no inner ringway should be built, and rather vague reference was made to the need for roads elsewhere. Instead, the policy was to keep London Transport fares down, improve bus and tube services, and deter people from using their cars as much as possible. It was a philosophy appropriate to the fashion of the day, which was to abhor the environmental consequences of motorways and enthuse over the social benefits of public transport.

Promises, promises

Labour had not always felt this way. The GLC manifestos of the past ten years show that transport planning owes as much to politicians' attempts to ride the swings of fashion for electoral advantage, as to any coherent philosophy. After launching the road plans for London in 1965, Labour stuck to its guns for the 1967 election:

> Today there are over a million cars in Greater London. By 1980 there will be two million. A new and efficient network of roads which will divert traffic from busy shopping streets and residential areas onto roads for the motor age is being created.
>
> The priorities are for circular roads in Outer London. As well as improvements to the over-worked North Circular Road, the GLC is planning a new South Circular Road. In addition, there will also be a modern D-ring road even further out. To draw off traffic from the residential areas and make them quieter and

safer, Labour is planning a motorway box around Inner London and work is already going on.

In that and the following election of 1970, both won by the Tories, the parties were in broad agreement on road building. For the 1973 election, the Tory leader, Desmond Plummer, promised to amalgamate two of the inner ringways, but was still in favour of a major road programme. On the other hand, Labour had changed course entirely, and was even denying parentage of the road plans:

> It (Labour) rejects the reckless and irrelevant Tory plan for ringways. They would attract more traffic and add to the congestion. Labour would spend the £2,000,000,000 saved from scrapping the Tory scheme on clearing the road chaos, especially by boosting public transport.

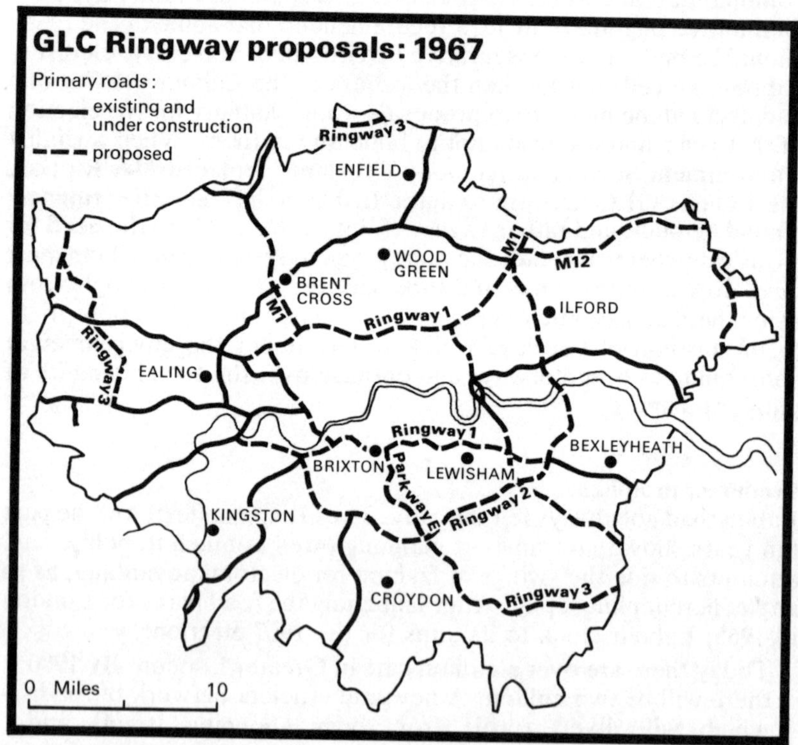

Source: Taken from *London's Roads — The Council's Objectives* (November, 1967)

Note: The above map indicates only proposals for roads within the Greater London area. As a result, much of Ringway 3 is not included as most of it fell outside the Greater London boundary.

As the GLC Labour politicians are now well aware, the £2,000 million was not theirs to spend. It lay in paper plans, rather than the coffers of County Hall. In May 1973 Labour won an overwhelming majority in County Hall. Following a gradual process of revoking all major road schemes formerly adopted by the Tories, the Labour GLC disposed of the last remaining link with Abercrombie's vision for easy movement in London when, on 8 December 1976, the northern section of Ringway 1 was abandoned. A press notice, headed 'GLC buries last of the ringways', quoted Enid Wistrich, chairman of the GLC's Central Area Board, as saying, 'At last we can say "Good riddance" to the last of these outdated and destructive roads'.

Who pays, who benefits?

In its GLC election campaign for 1977, Labour promised to maintain subsidies to London Transport, attempt to transfer more freight to rail and water, and build the River Line tube through Docklands. Roads were mentioned only in terms of restraint, safety and the need for more cuts in building programmes. This current stance on transport fits the Left tradition of favouring collectivist rather than individualist policies. In this there are strong parallels between transport and housing. Home and car ownership are both equated: by supporters, with freedom of choice; by detractors in the inner areas with squeezing working-class tenants out of their rented homes through gentrification, or trapping buses in jams. There is a strong feeling in the Labour Party that council housing and public transport are intrinsically virtuous, yet electoral pragmatism dictated until fairly recently that deference should be shown to the strong individual desire of voters to own homes and cars.

Many of the policy issues can be cast in the same form: should council housing and public transport be a service for the community as a whole for those who cannot provide for themselves? Should fares/rents cover costs, with subsidies paid directly to those who cannot afford them? Should transport policy be directed mainly to aiding economic growth, by ensuring that people get to work easily and freight moves smoothly? Should homes go first to those who contribute most to the economic efficiency of the city? Or should top priority be ensuring that homeless single parent families are housed, and old age pensioners can get to the shops and bingo? One major difference between housing and transport is that cars are more available than homes. They are cheaper to buy and their production is not restricted by Government. While builders have to buy land, then seek planning permission before constructing homes, car manufacturers do not have to guarantee road or parking space. Governments, which monopolise road building, have failed to provide the additional roads needed to match the growth of car ownership in Britain from one million to seventeen million over the last thirty years. So while there are large numbers of new cars and cheap old bangers on congested roads, homes are costly and scarce.

However, no one disagrees that the swing to car use raises both environmental and social issues. Even if four out of five households own a car, there is still a need for a substantial public transport network in London – for two quite distinct reasons. First, as a viable and acceptable alternative to the private car, so people travelling to central London (and to the main suburban centres as well) do not feel their only option is to drive a car – or get out of London altogether. Second, as an essential service for those without access to a car, who are more numerous than the stereotype categories of children and the elderly: not only will a significant proportion of households never own cars, but most members of car owning households do not actually have access to the household car. Car owning households generate nearly as many public transport journeys as car journeys. The trick that nobody has managed to pull off is to provide a cheap and extensive public transport system when not many people are paying to use it. Either you have to pay to maintain a minimal service which breaks even, or taxpayers and ratepayers must provide a substantial subsidy.

So who pays? What should be the balance between fares and subsidy? In 1977, seventy-three per cent of London Transport's costs will be met by fares and other income. The year of heaviest subsidy was 1975 when fares, etc. covered only sixty-two per cent of costs. But even then the subsidy level was substantially lower than in most other major European cities. In Paris, for instance, fares covered only one third, and in New York and Tokyo less than half of total costs. In Paris, in particular, millions are being poured into expanding their underground system. As well as building roads, the French are investing £400 million a year in public transport, quite apart from subsidies, compared with £60-£70 million by London Transport. Just what balance of public and private transport may be appropriate for London is discussed later in terms of the way people want to travel, and the resources available to meet that demand. There are those who would say debate is irrelevant and that we will not have much choice over transport policy in the future because, instead of simply trying to save public money, we will have to save energy.

The crude argument is that since there may be an oil and petrol shortage by the time today's children are middle-aged, it is crazy to build more roads for cars. We should be going all out to maintain and improve public transport, and redesign our towns and cities so that people have to travel as little as possible between their homes and jobs. The corner shop should be preserved, the out-of-town drive-in supermarket banned. The problem lies in persuading today's parents that they should forsake the joys of driving the kids to the seaside, so that when the children grow up they will still have a decent train service to Southend. The counter argument is that we are already locked into a life-style which depends upon personal mobility, not just for pleasure, but for economic survival. Already a substantial proportion of people drive to work in London because their jobs are outside the centre. About ninety per cent of freight goes by road, and whatever the environmental benefit of barges and goods wagons, you cannot get either into Oxford Street. Nor can you take bags of cement by tube.

The roads lobby points out that the best way to save petrol is to build some decent roads so that journeys are speeded up, and cars and lorries do not have to use up valuable fuel stuck in jams. One major form of public transport, buses, uses roads and oil. Even if we do run out of petrol, the demand for personal mobility will be so great that electric cars will be snapped up, despite having to remember to plug them in for an overnight recharge. That does not mean an orgy of road building which would attract more traffic—just that there is a case for limited construction. In the short term, energy can probably only be conserved by Government measures to ration fuel or increase prices. This would be both extremely unpopular and would help price British goods out of the world market. Therefore it is realistic to discuss the choices we have about travel in the 1980s and 1990s. Two factors dominate the argument: the way people want to travel, and the resources which will be available to build roads or improve public transport.

HOW PEOPLE GET TO WORK IN CENTRAL LONDON

	1961	1966	1971	1972	1973	1974	1975
British Rail	452	456	460	442	435	419	403
LT rail (less BR transfers)	430	416	385	381	370	375	344
LT bus	209	175	146	144	144	143	148
Total public transport	**1,090**	**1,047**	**991**	**967**	**949**	**937**	**895**
Total Private* Transport	174	166	174	185	188	183	181

*Includes a proportion of through traffic.

All figures to nearest thousand passenger arrivals.

Based on peak period travel 0700 – 1000 hours.

Source: Annual Abstract of Greater London statistics.

Source of 1975 figures: British Rail, London Transport, GLC.

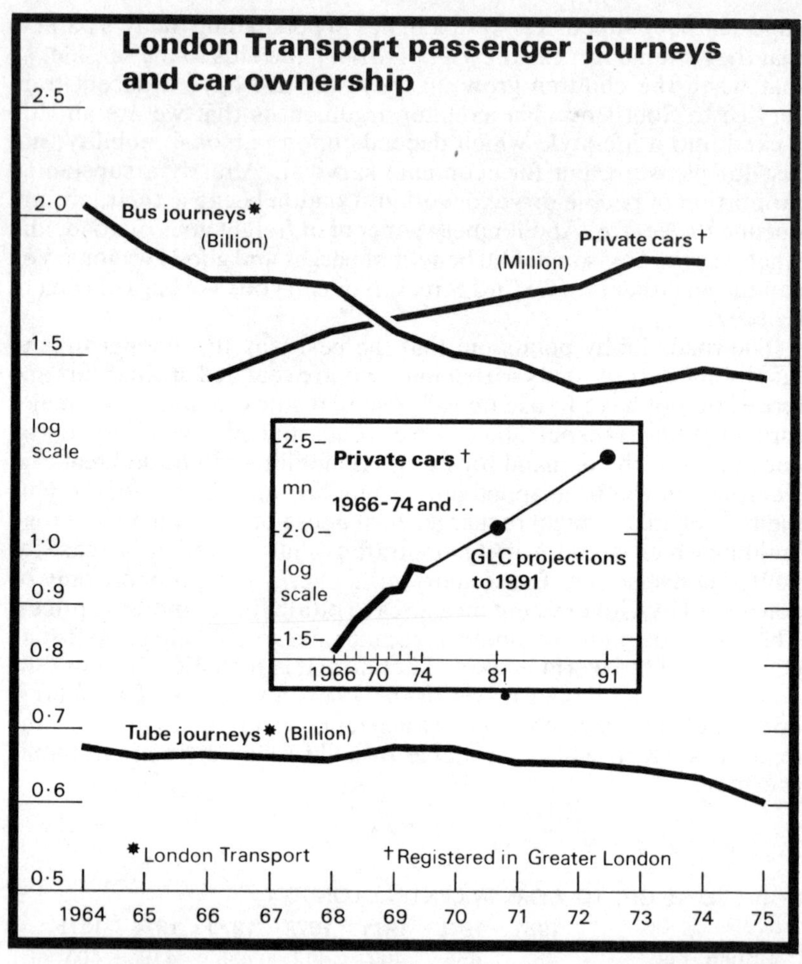

Source: LT figures: Annual reports, London Transport Executive. Car ownership: Department of the Environment and GLC Director-General's Department.

Note: There are many more journeys taken on London Transport than there are cars owned by Londoners. The use of a log scale enables a direct comparison to be made between the trends of using public transport and of owning cars.

How Londoners travel

The 1971 census showed that more Londoners drove to work than went by bus or rail. About one-sixth walked. Broadly speaking, long-distance commuters are using rail, people in inner London use cars, buses and tubes, while in outer London well over a third of the workers drive to their jobs. This picture makes Labour's policy look rather bizarre, and future trends are even more at odds with it for, as the census showed, as car ownership rises more people leave public transport and drive to work — particularly in outer London where public transport is less satisfactory and cross-country trips relatively difficult. This trend will increase as car ownership expands in the suburbs in the 1980s, yet the GLC has actually accelerated it by restricting office building in central London (where commuting by public transport would be relatively easy) and instead encouraging dispersal to suburban centres. Unless public transport to these suburban centres is improved by reorganising bus services, building some relief roads and restraining car use, more and more people will drive to work. So far there is little evidence that the GLC has woken up to the fact that each major suburban office and shopping centre is equivalent to a Nottingham, Leicester or Bradford, and needs a similar transport policy. Car use has increased even more for the other trips people make, like shopping, taking the kids to school, or visiting granny. By the 1990s, five families in seven are expected to own cars in London, with the figure as high as four in five in the suburbs.

These forecasts can, of course, be challenged. It may be argued that if enough is spent on maintaining and improving public transport, people will take the bus or train, forego the car and save their money. To some extent they will — but the desire to own and use a car is strong. A survey done by MIL Research Ltd in 1976 showed that in the South East, fifty-two per cent of car owners felt their car absolutely essential. Forty-one per cent said they would have to change their job if they lost their car, nineteen per cent that they would have to move house, fifty-six per cent that they would have to rearrange their social life. Thirty per cent said they used their car for work. Only thirty-six per cent said they would use their car less if public transport were improved. The research was done for the Society of Motor Manufacturers, but I do not think the results reflect just wishful thinking on their part. One estimate given by the GLC's chief transportation planner, David Bayliss, is that traffic in London would reduce by only twenty per cent overall if public transport were free, if there were also substantially better services and selective traffic restraint. Increasing public transport services up to thirty per cent, or cutting fares by the same amount is only likely to increase demand by ten per cent. Any shift to public transport which reduces road congestion is worthwhile, but the move towards increased car use cannot be ignored.

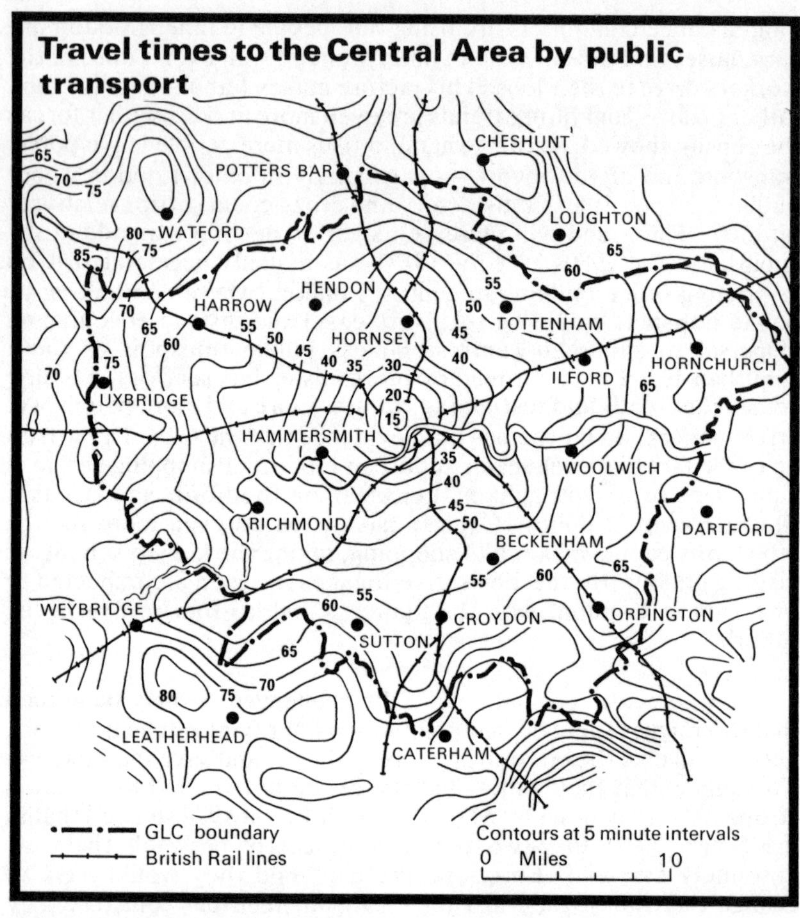

Source: Adapted from *Greater London Intelligence Quarterly,* March 1974.

The hollow ring

While there is evidence to suggest that you can do something to deter people from switching away from public transport by using subsidies to hold fares down, you cannot expect to keep people in London against their expectations of being able increasingly to use their cars for work and leisure. London is spreading gradually outwards as people move from inner London to the suburbs and beyond, and those in the suburbs move further into the countryside. As the workers move out, so do the jobs. Industry has left the inner area for sites in Slough and Reading, Basildon and Crawley. Offices have moved clerical staff from the city to the suburbs, and further out. The move of office jobs has been reflected in the commuting figures. The peak for commuting from inner London to the centre was reached in the early 1960s, and by the middle 1970s had dropped by twenty five per cent. Outer suburban commuting peaked in 1971, and long-distance commuting has fallen since 1973. By 1991 overall commuting from all destinations to central London is expected to have fallen still further.

So it is not just a case of people living further out and then travelling longer distances back into work. The living and working pattern of London is gradually changing. As people buy cars, they change the way they use the city, and in doing so change its structure. Once people have moved out to Epsom, they almost certainly own a car and prefer to drive to work in Kingston or Croydon. The GLC policy of concentrating offices in suburban centres without providing considerably improved public transport to them reinforces the trend. The traditional pattern of suburban commuters travelling into the centre is being replaced by the ring city around London, an ever-thickening hollow doughnut encompassing New and Expanding Towns like Basildon, Bracknell, Crawley, Harlow, Hatfield, Hemel Hempstead, Stevenage and Welwyn Garden City.

Because of this dominant trend, the transport planners are faced with a particularly difficult choice: do they try to row against the current by doing everything possible to maintain and improve public transport within London, in the belief that this will ensure good services for the substantial minority without access to cars, and also preserve the vital links between jobs in the centre and homes? This would help ensure that the economic base of the centre is not threatened; but it would inevitably mean spending millions of pounds of the taxpayers' and ratepayers' money each year on maintaining public transport services. Or do transport planners concede that the outward trend is here to stay, and the best policy is to work with it? In this case, public transport would be maintained for commuting and getting to suburban centres, and as a social service, but careful scrutiny given to the level of subsidy and investment. Improvements would be made where they attract most extra fare-paying passengers, or where there is a strong social need. Road building would not be neglected. Instead of concentrating all new roads outside London, so reinforcing the ring city, some consideration would be given to car travel within suburban London. What makes no sense is to disperse offices to suburban centres, then to provide neither good public transport nor some road improvements.

Salaries and subsidies

On this analysis, the issue is not roads versus public transport, but achieving the best balance so that each performs the function to which it is best suited. Public transport is good at moving large numbers of people in and out of the centre, and essential for a substantial minority without cars. Unless suburban families have two cars, many members of the household will continue to depend on buses and trains. Cars are a great nuisance to everyone else if driven into the centre, but are particularly convenient for many trips around the suburbs and the edge of London. A ring-rail system would not have the same effect unless everyone lived and worked within a few minutes walk of a station; otherwise they would be obliged to drive to the station or take a bus, and do the same at the other end.

Although public and private transport may be complementary, tough decisions must be taken on the relative balance of spending. Before getting to the major issue of the amount of money which will be available for transport over the next ten to fifteen years, two recent examples serve to show how politicians have found decisions on transport spending difficult. The GLC controls most of inner London's main road building as well as London Transport, whereas British Rail is directly responsible to central Government. The Labour GLC administration began a campaign in 1976 to bring London British Rail services under its own control, but it is unlikely that the Government will agree to substantial changes yet. So, for now at least, commuters facing fare increases must direct their anger at the Transport Secretary.

So far, the Government has maintained that there can be no increase in the £60 million a year given to British Rail to keep down fares on the London commuter network, and no increase in the level of capital spending necessary to carry out electrification and other improvements to services. Between 1971 and 1976 fares have risen by 150 per cent, and over the next five years further increases are inevitable because the government maintains that long-distance commuters, in particular, are relatively well-off and could afford higher fares. British Rail has calculated that Government policy would mean fare rises of seven and a half per cent a year on top of inflation. British Rail and the rail unions maintain that this could produce severe problems on two counts. First, rises of that order could mean a fifteen per cent loss of passengers, not all because of a simple switch to cars. However, past calculations show that a mere five per cent transfer of trips bound for central London from rail to road leads to a twenty per cent increase in peak-hour traffic and, consequently, more congestion. Secondly, if people find it too expensive to travel to work in the centre they will press for higher wages or look for work locally, so increasing pressure on firms to move out of London. The counter argument is that people are tending to leave jobs in central London anyway, and the trends suggest fewer and fewer commuters whatever the fare levels. So surely it does not make sense to keep on pouring money into a declining service when the funds could be used better elsewhere? Fare increases have not yet reached the point where the rise brings in less money because fewer people travel. In 1975 fare increases of fifty per cent produced ridership losses of only five per cent, so there seems plenty of scope for big rises.

However, plausible as these arguments may seem, they only tell half the story. People do not suddenly decide they will not go to work any more because they cannot afford the fare. If fares become too much of a burden, they will, given time, find opportunities for jobs which do not entail commuting into central London. The natural turnover of homes and jobs means that it takes at least two, and possibly as much as five years or more for effects to work through. Viewed in this light, an immediate five per cent loss may be cause for alarm as it implies far greater passenger loss in the longer term. The cumulative effects of a succession of hefty fare increases is likely to be even greater. At the time of writing we await a Government announcement following consultation on its 1976 Transport Policy Review, which sets out the likely constraints on spending.

The problems of London Transport have proved just as intractable for politicians of both parties since County Hall took charge in 1970. The Tory GLC under Desmond Plummer only agreed to take on London Transport from the Transport Ministry on the condition that past debts were written off and that the Government raised fares to produce a surplus in the first year. Plummer said, 'We're here to provide a transportation system, not a welfare service . . . I believe you must stick to the commercial attitude, otherwise you are on a slippery slope . . . If a deficit is running one year it will have to be made up the next.' Plummer said that capital grants for new buses and trains or other improvements were acceptable, but not revenue subsidies.

The Tories soon found that they could not run London Transport at a profit. By 1972, the year before a GLC election, a major fare rise was needed to break even for that year. Instead, the chairman of the Policy and Resources Committee, Horace Cutler, announced a reduced fare rise and an asset replacement grant. On the basis that grants were fine, but subsidies just welfare hand-outs, that sounded all right. In fact, the grant was a disguised subsidy from the rates because it helped balance the revenue account by reducing the amount allowed for asset depreciation. Mr Plummer's promise of no subsidy had been broken in two years, despite the attempt at concealment. In March 1972, the London Regional Conference of the Labour Party had voted in favour of charging no fares on London Transport, and paying all costs from the rates. When Labour did gain control of County Hall in 1973, they took a more cautious line and simply promised to hold fares down (which they managed to do for another two years). Old age pensioners were given free travel passes on off-peak buses, and children a flat fare on the buses, but by 1975 fare rises were deemed necessary to avoid enormous rate increases. Inflation and a very generous pay rise for transport workers aimed at recruiting more staff had proved more than a match for political idealism.

Between 1972 and Spring 1977, bus and tube fares rose overall by 100 per cent and yet the GLC and Government will still need to subsidise London Transport to the tune of £90 million in 1977 to enable it to break even plus another fare increase in the summer of 1977. In the previous four years the subsidies have been £18 million, £43 million, £116 million and £114 million in cash terms, which would be higher on today's price base. It is tempting to say that the fare rises have been shocking and the subsidies a disastrous waste of money, but the fare increases are not quite so horrific when compared with other costs. Bus fares have not risen substantially in real terms, and tube fares gone up only ten to fifteen per cent more than other prices. Furthermore, it is too simplistic to say that subsidies are bad, and grants are good.

Conventional economic wisdom, or at least that of the Department of Transport and the Tories, is that grants to build a new tube line, replace old trains and buses, or improve stations are sound investment, while subsidies will sap the managerial efficiency of the organisation and are only of transient benefit. London Transport, on the other hand, maintains that if subsidies are firmly set in advance – instead of being added to cover any deficits – there is no loss of managerial control. The important question is how to get the best value out of the money being spent: whether it is on paying busmen's wages or buying new trains for the Northern Line. If there is not a staff shortage, but the trains are always breaking down, it will be better to buy new trains; again, financed by the taxpayers or ratepayers or through borrowing, with the interest paid from the fare receipts. But if there is a staff shortage, more trains are little help; it is better to spend money on recruitment. Seen in this way there is not really much difference between grants and subsidies. It is all money to the GLC, although there are finer economic arguments about resource consumption, depending on how subsidies and grants are spent.

In order to compare different projects, value for money is measured in extra passenger miles travelled per pound spent; that is, how many extra travellers you attract for additional funds laid out, whether in grant or subsidy. In 1973, it was better value for money to increase bus and rail services than to hold fares down. At first the Labour GLC used subsidies to hold fares down, but later raised them

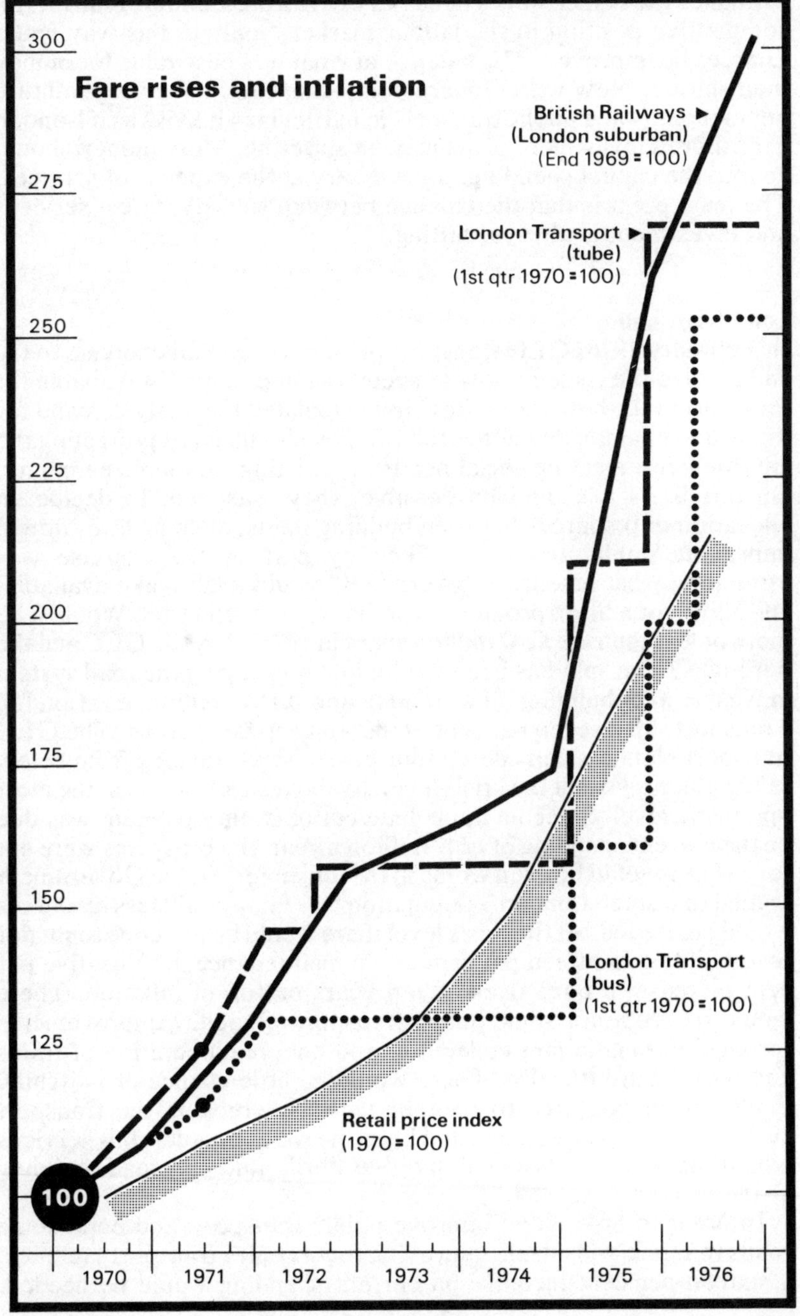
Fare rises and inflation
300
275
250
225
200
175
150
125
100
British Railways ▶
(London suburban)
(End 1969 = 100)
London Transport ▶
(tube)
(1st qtr 1970 = 100)
London Transport
(bus)
(1st qtr 1970 = 100)
Retail price index
(1970 = 100)
1970
1971
1972
1973
1974
1975
1976

to finance the higher wages necessary to restore London Transport's competitive position in the labour market – only in this way could services be improved. The balance of what was best value for money then shifted. Now with Government squeezing, public expenditure on transport – and public transport in particular – it looks as if London Transport's investment plans may be suffering. More money should go into the capital spending, if necessary at the expense of services. The main point is that the balance between subsidy, fares, services and investment is always shifting.

Long term policy

In February 1976, GLC transport planners began an exercise to try and resolve the issue of how to spend the limited funds available for transport in the best way. They first calculated the likely demand for travel and examined whether top priority should go to protecting the environment, meeting social needs or assisting London's economy. On this basis it should be possible, they reasoned, to decide an allocation of resources between building roads, keeping fares down, improving public transport. The key part of the exercise was estimating what resources government would itself make available, and allow councils to provide, over the next fifteen years. Would it be more or less than the £247 million spent in 1976/77 by the GLC and the boroughs? The split has been £93 million on keeping the road system in shape and building new roads, and £154 million on London Transport, fifty-seven per cent of that to keep fares down. The GLC transport planners considered four possibilities, ranging from below £170 million a year at the crisis level, to above £280 million at the most optimistic level. Since an immediate cut of twenty per cent was due on the current spending of £247 million a year, the prospects were not rosy. They would be even worse in the longer term if the Government argued that since London's population was falling, still less resources would be needed. At the crisis level there would be no scope for major road building, a fifteen per cent cut in maintenance, a thirty-five per cent increase in fares over fifteen years on top of inflation. There would be scope for some public transport efficiency improvements through automatic fare collection, and one man operation of trains and buses, but little else. There would be little chance of switching money from one area to another without wrecking the transport system. To keep fares down and keep the roads in order, bus services would have to be slashed by one-third, and all road building abandoned.

In order to hold fares, improve public transport, and build some roads in Docklands while improving town centre transport facilities, a sixteen per cent increase on current spending would be needed.

That would still not leave room for the £200 million River Line tube through Docklands which would have to be financed separately. The basic conclusion to emerge from the study was that to avoid deterioration of the transport system about £3,500 million was needed over the next fifteen years, representing only a small cut on current expenditure. That would allow some decisions to be taken on whether to hold fares down or to build roads, for example. On the prudent assumption that spending is not likely to exceed £3,000 million over fifteen years, some fairly firm guidelines for policy can be established. First, unless fares are increased by fifty per cent above inflation, or bus services slashed, some subsidies will be needed for public transport. Second, there will not be the funds to carry out any major road building programmes. The Rochester Way relief road in South East London and the South Woodford to Barking relief north of the River may be built, but the new East London river crossing at Thamesmead to link them may be in doubt. There is little prospect of the £60 million Thames tunnel to relieve Tower Bridge, or the £80 million southern relief road through Docklands, designed to relieve Greenwich by taking traffic from Woolwich across the Thames to the Isle of Dogs and on to Surrey Docks.

The M25 motorway around London, however, will be built. Since it falls outside the GLC boundary and offers some small hope of diverting lorries without knocking down the homes of GLC voters, the council is in favour of it, and the Department of Transport is determined to press ahead and finish the scheme by 1983. Radial routes such as the M11 will plug the rest of the national motorway network into the M25. The Labour politicians at the GLC do not seem to have realised, though, that the M25 could act as a powerful magnet around London, sucking out more firms looking for cheap sites with easy connections to the rest of the country, reinforcing the ring city and eating away at its heart.

Making the best of it

From the financial analysis it appears that there is little room for maneouvre. Both grandiose motorway schemes and tube extensions are out of the question and more attention will have to be devoted to making better use of the existing system.

On the roads this means some form of restraint on inessential traffic leaving space for buses and commercial traffic. The first moves towards car restraint were made in Mayfair in 1958 with the introduction of parking meters. Since then, off-street parking lots have been closed down, garage charges raised, and the GLC under Labour has sought legislation to allow it to stop car commuters using parks under office blocks (known as PNR, private non-residential parking). These restraint measures, together with one-way streets and other management schemes, have kept traffic speeds in central London fairly consistent, while traffic itself has increased fifty per cent since 1962. The petrol price rise from thirty-five pence to over seventy pence in two years produced a temporary halt to traffic growth, but there is now a slow increase.

The theoretical aim of more controls on central London traffic is admirable. The GLC estimates that if traffic were cut by a third a variety of benefits could follow:

Bus journey times could be reduced by thirty per cent; traffic speeds increased by up to forty per cent; traffic reduced in residential streets; and preference given to essential deliveries. However, parking controls alone will not achieve those large reductions in traffic. The trouble is that through traffic has doubled since 1962, taking up road space created by the parking curbs on commuters. Ever since the Smeed Committee reported, there has been talk of road pricing, that is, charging cars for the roads they use by a taxi-type meter or similar device, to reduce through traffic. Detailed work has also been carried out on the possibility of introducing supplementary licencing, under which drivers would have to buy a special licence for £1.50 or more to allow them to drive in the centre. Since Labour politicians do not like a scheme which they feel might hit the poorer driver, Camden Council has suggested licences which could be handed out according to the need of the driver.

There are obvious difficulties in actually introducing these schemes, not least the need to employ hundreds of extra traffic wardens. There is a danger that while the central area would become less congested, the ring immediately around would become more so. Furthermore, no one knows for sure what effect additional restraint would have on shops and small businesses which are already operating on the borderline. If they lost customers, will there be a flood of closures? Westminster Council is opposed to further restraint for this reason. City engineer, Alan Cryer, says:

> It looks as if we are going to have a siege economy in this country for the next five years, and business houses are pleading with planners not to make life more difficult for them. Some of the PNR space may just be contributing to laziness, used by people who could come in by public transport. But I get the message that in many cases a parking space may be the way that a firm retains a key member of staff who would not otherwise be prepared to work in London.

The Labour controlled London Boroughs Association agrees and has written to the GLC opposing their control scheme on the basis that it could damage London's economy.

Public transport

What are the possibilities and problems for London Transport? If there is not going to be much to spend on holding fares or carrying out major investment, it is all the more important to make the best use of what is there – and make it as attractive as possible. There are some bright spots – in spite of everything, the tubes still operate a pretty good service (the tourists think so too), although the fares look high to the Londoner with his shrinking purse. London Transport's marketing is a bit more confident and outgoing, and has helped to prevent the recent astronomical fares increases driving more than five to ten per cent of the traffic away. Staff shortages on the buses and tubes have been largely overcome, though the high wages that have achieved this now mean London Transport cannot afford to operate the full bus timetable. They have not the money to employ more highly-paid staff. Only more productivity can stem the remorseless upward trend in costs. One-man trains and automatic ticketing barriers to save ticket collectors on the tubes are firmly planned – but investment is needed to achieve this. More one-man buses hold the prospect of saving several thousand conductors but need better and faster methods of pay-on-entry to overcome the delays at stops. London Transport's pre-paid ticket system (introduced experimentally in Havering in the summer of 1977) may hold the answer.

The main problem is the bus service itself. For years LT has protested that the big problem is traffic congestion: if only those cars, taxis and lorries didn't get in the way they would run a reliable service. On this basis the GLC has introduced over 140 bus-only lanes to try and carve a path through the jams, and helped in other ways to give buses priority. These have been successful locally, and where several bus lanes have been strung along a whole bus route, the improvement has been more substantial. But generally, the truth of the matter is more complicated. Studies done by GLC and London Transport show that mechanical failure of buses and problems of control are just as much to blame for irregularity as congestion. In short, buses do not just get held up on the route, they often do not leave the terminus on time – or at all, if the buses break down. London Transport maintains that over the last ten years, Government policy on giving bus grants only on standardised buses meant it was forced to buy buses unsuitable for London.

At last it looks as if London Transport may be getting on top of the mechanical problems, although the price is throwing out some of the early single deckers after less than seven years. Meanwhile, bus radio and, particularly, the equipping of a third of the roadside inspectors with pocket radios is making the control of the routes more effective and more flexible. Naturally, London Transport is rather cagey about its day-to-day problems. It is difficult for the GLC to discover whether the problems are caused by union rules or inefficient management. It is just as difficult to discover how British Rail operates services and whether there is scope for improvement. At least the public can try to get some satisfaction over London Transport by prodding the GLC into action. British Rail is almost a complete mystery. There is no publicly accountable forum of debate where the virtue of electrification schemes, manning arrangements, station improvements can be discussed. The two rail empires of London Transport and British Rail are still run in isolation, despite various liaison committees.

Who's in charge?

Two main conclusions emerge from this analysis. First, planners and politicians must come to terms with what is happening to London and decide how far they wish to swing with the trend or oppose it. Second, there must be clearer definition of who is going to carry out whatever policies are necessary. So far, evidence of the forces which shape London has not been made available to the public in comprehensible form. What work has been done on precisely why people and firms leave London, and the policies which would make them change their minds? If the work has not been done, it should be. Until these issues are resolved it is crazy to spend haphazardly on public transport or road building, or cut without logic on the whim of whichever party is in control. Secondly, Londoners have the right to demand an end to the shadow boxing which takes place between GLC and the Department of Transport. The Government has indicated, for example, that it thinks a major new road is needed in London. Anthony Crosland, when Environment Secretary, conveniently pointed this out in the map he included in his 1976 judgement on the Layfield Inquiry into the Greater London Development Plan. It would have been politically most embarrassing actually to draw in a road when the Labour GLC had promised not to build any motorways, so Mr Crosland dotted in some points, between which it was difficult to drive, and which would benefit from connection. Anyone bold enough to join the dots finds a new substitute for the South Circular road, which currently exists only as a string of sign posts. A new road would have the benefit of relieving congested residential streets, allowing the M23 to be continued north to the Streatham area, but most important, offering some hope of keeping, if not re-establishing, industry in areas with some of the highest rates of unemployment in London.

However, under the present finance system the money is not available to build the roads. The Government is pressing ahead with improvements to the North Circular and the M25, which are their

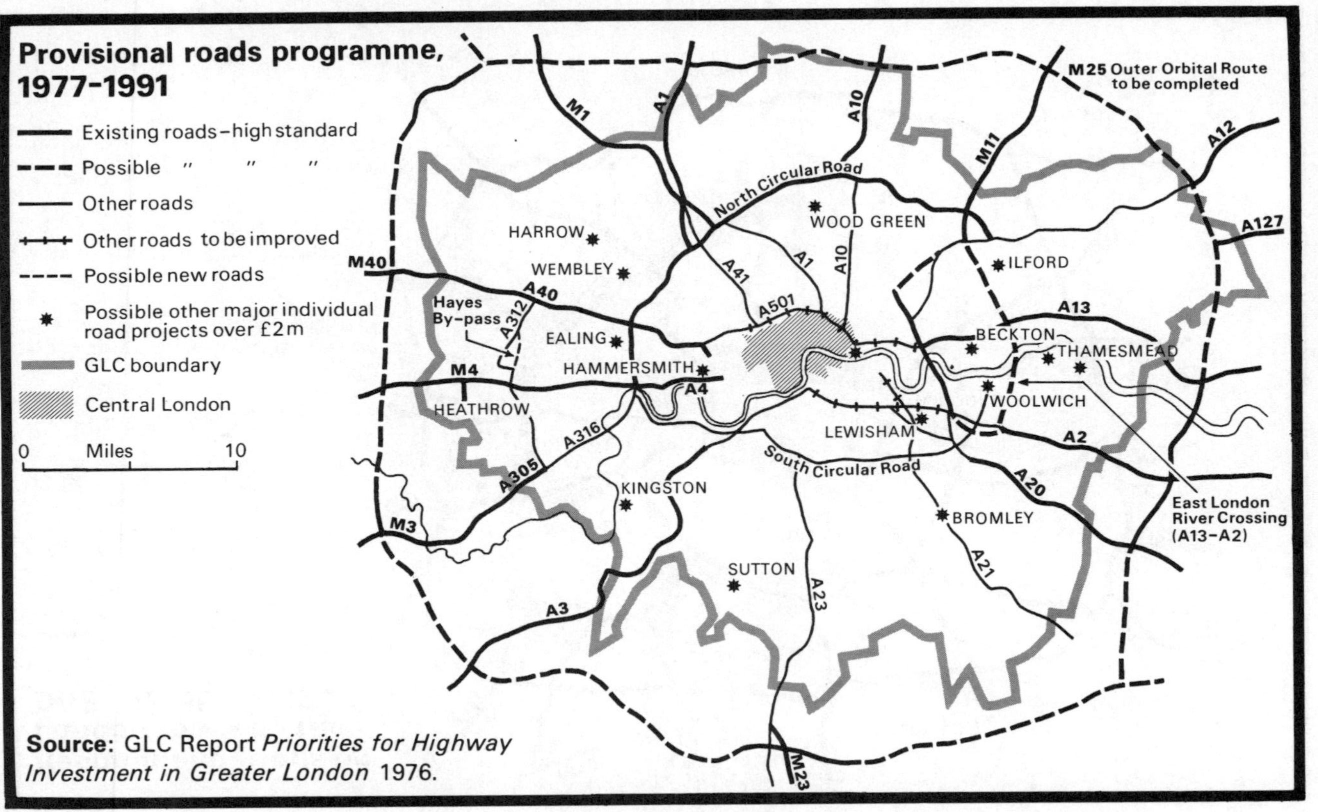

Source: GLC Report *Priorities for Highway Investment in Greater London* 1976.

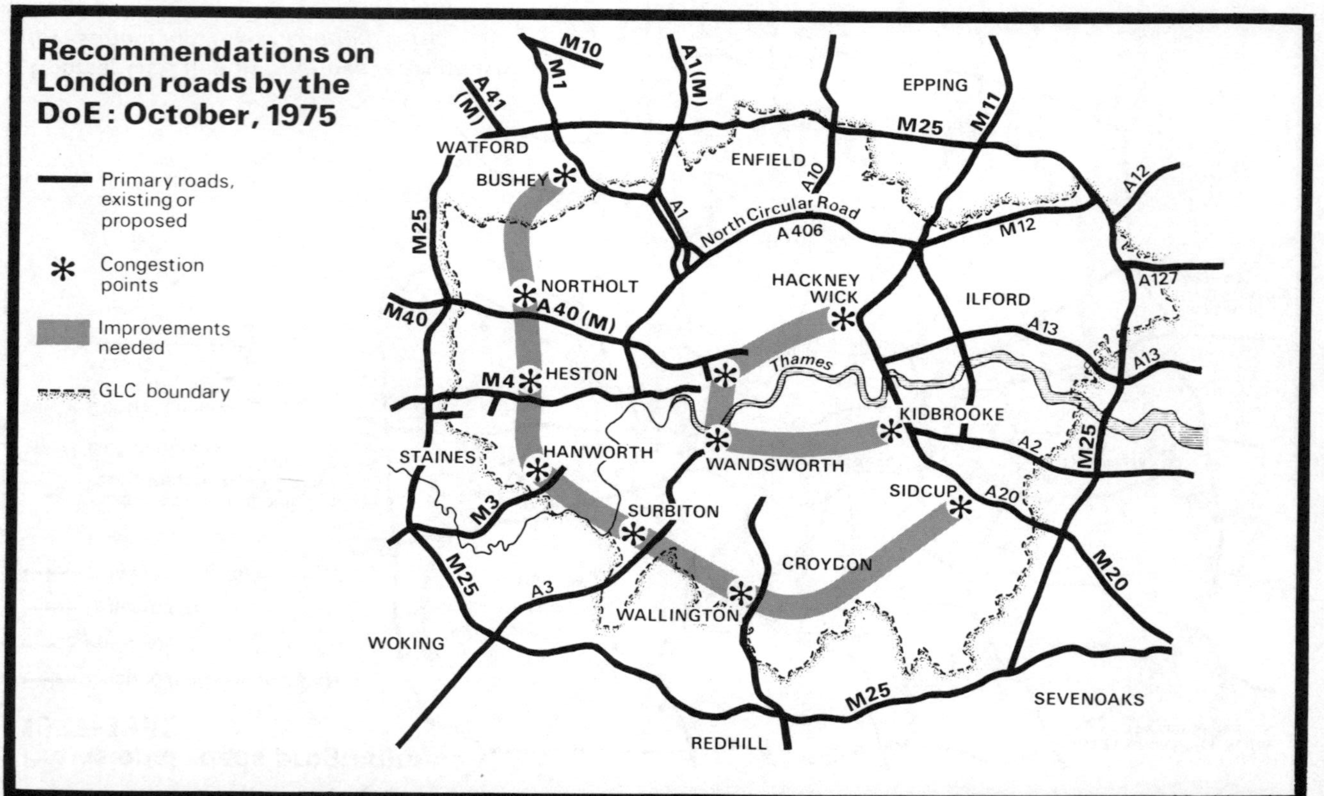

Recommendations on London roads by the DoE: October, 1975

responsibility, but the GLC could only do the southern arc by diverting funds from public transport and probably wrecking the system. Why should the Department of Transport not be responsible for all major roads within London? If major roads in London are judged necessary, then they are of national importance. Furthermore, they can only be built by Government: the changing political control of County Hall and boroughs ensures that it is impossible for local government to carry any controversial scheme through to completion. The division of responsibility between the GLC and Government for running London Transport and British Rail services means that Londoners are denied both any overall transport plans and some relatively minor improvements which would be welcome. The London Rail Advisory Committee, which is meant to bridge the gap between London Transport, British Rail, Greater London Council and Government has achieved nothing so far. At present, it is impossible to agree simple matters like season tickets which cover both British Rail services and tubes or buses, and advertising of services. There is far too little concern given to improvement of interchanges between British Rail and London Transport services. If the Government is not prepared to give the GLC some control over British Rail it should produce alternative proposals for integrating the two public transport empires and ensure some common policy objectives for the GLC and Department of Transport.

But London's transport needs are so infinitely complex, and rely so much on intelligent forecasting combined with sympathy for public aspirations, that they will probably need a new strategic authority one day. Imagine a Greater London Movement Board, financed by Central and local government grant, with democratic and representative elements (CBI, TUC, GLC, etc) in its make-up – but operating independently in control of rail, tube, buses, road-building and private car control. Futuristic. Impossible, maybe. But at least you'd know who to blame.

Suggested reading

The Growth of Victorian London, Donald Olsen (Batsford 1976)

A History of London Transport (2 Volumes), T. C. Barker and M. Robbins (Allen and Unwin 1974)

Strategic Planning in London, Douglas A. Hart (Pergammon 1976) Deals with the conflicts over the primary roads' network.

Transport Organisation in a Great City – the case of London, Michael Collins and Timothy Pharoah (Allen and Unwin 1974).

Transport Realities and Planning Policy, Mayer Hillman, Irwin Henderson and Anne Walley (PEP 1976)

Planning for Public Transport, Peter White (Hutchinson 1976)

Moving in Cities, Brian Richards (Cassell and Collier Macmillan 1976)

Motorways in London, J. Michael Thomson (Gerald Duckworth 1969)

Instead of Cars, Terence Bendixson (Temple Smith 1974)
Economics and Transport Policy, K. M. Gwilliam and P. J. Mackie. (Allen and Unwin 1975)
The Train That Ran Away, Stewart Joy (Ian Allen Ltd. 1973)
Rail Problems: an Alternative Strategy, Pryke and Dodgson (Martin Robertson 1975)
Strategy for the South East: 1976 Review, Transport report (Department of the Environment 1976)

FINDING A HOME

Since the Second World War, when so much of London's housing was destroyed, councils have spent enormous sums of money on building over 500,000 new houses and buying and renovating older ones; and private developers have added about 200,000 homes. Meanwhile, the city's population has dropped by 1,170,000 since 1951 and there is at last the apparent prospect of no housing shortage in London: the number of homes is virtually the same as the number of households. And yet, during the past twelve years the number of people on council house waiting lists has risen from 152,000 to over 200,000. By the end of 1976, 15,000 families were recognised as homeless. Home ownership is beyond the reach of most people, and renting a flat privately is extremely difficult and expensive.

This perplexing paradox, in which there is no housing shortage on the one hand, yet on the other, more people than ever seem dissatisfied with their accommodation – or are actually homeless – lies at the heart of London's housing dilemma. Part of the trouble is that households are made up of varying numbers and ages of people, whose needs, incomes and aspirations differ; just as houses come in many different sizes, locations, conditions and prices. And although the total number of people in London has dropped dramatically, the number of households has fallen far less. Families are smaller and more people live alone. Nevertheless, with so much concern on the part of politicians to match home to household, the London housing situation should be improving. Instead, a jumble of legislation, rapid swings of policy and chaotic subsidies have created total confusion and many inequalities.

Both those who supply housing and those who are looking for it complain that the other side is to blame. Councils say that families on the waiting list are too choosy, and indeed local authorities have been forced to start letting older property on a first-come first-served basis to any young couples prepared to accept lower standards. Landlords say that tenants have too many rights, and consequently owners are keeping property empty in the hope of selling, rather than letting. Building societies are accused of failing to lend on older property or conversion. An army of 10,000 squatters has decided that direct action is the only way to break the log-jam.

The squatters and the homeless catch the headlines, but tens of thousands more are nearly as desperate. These 'hidden homeless' are seen daily by the many housing aid centres set up over the past few years. Nick Raynsford, director of SHAC (The London Housing Aid Centre), presents a picture common to many similar voluntary and council-aided establishments:

> Most of the people who come to see us are young families, with one or two young children, and one or two parents aged between 18 and 30, earnings perhaps £50 to £60 a week. Typically they are living in furnished rented rooms, or sharing with parents or friends, and are desperate for a home of their own to escape overcrowding and high rents. Some are one-parent families – often young West Indian girls – who usually cannot work because they have to look after the child. Some of the families are literally homeless or facing eviction, but many more are the concealed homeless who haven't a home of their own but cannot get help directly from their local council. They may have their names on the waiting list but that doesn't offer much hope immediately. Decent private flats with two bedrooms are almost impossible to find at rents the people we see can afford. And most of these families don't earn enough to buy a house. They find it impossible to break into the housing system at any point.
>
> Even those who are actually homeless may not get much help from councils, who seem to think they are in some way undeserving and often accuse them of trying to jump the queue. Yet many of these may be on the council's waiting list and have become homeless because they have been thrown out of the place they were sharing with relatives or friends – perhaps when a child was born.

Of course, London's housing situation has got better in many ways. Much has been done to improve the overall condition of London's housing – fewer people lack kitchens and bathrooms, overcrowding is down to three per cent. The Rent Acts have ended the worst excesses of harassment and eviction, common in the Rachman era of the early 1960s. But all this, even coupled with the fact that there are more houses and less people than ever before, does not alter the fact that it is becoming more and more difficult for people to gain access to the housing system, or, once they are in it, to change homes if they wish to.

The growing queue

This paradox in the London housing situation can be illustrated by a loose analogy. Imagine a restaurant, which is popular because of the wide range of dishes it offers, yet frustrating for potential diners because the service is erratic and the tables badly arranged. Many of those already seated are clearly enjoying their food and have even managed to reserve seats at their tables for friends arriving later. Others are cramped and complaining about their neighbours and the state of the tablecloths. A few tables are reserved by the management, or waiting to be cleared; others are laid ready for new customers. A restless queue is growing at the door, getting little satisfaction because many are on their own or in twos, while most of the vacant tables are for family groups of four to six. The head waiter tries to persuade people into sharing, because the tables are pinned to the floor and cannot be shifted to suit the diners. To alleviate the situation, the management is instead constructing an expensive new annex to the restaurant in the hope that this will be finished before those in the queue collapse from hunger or leave in search of food elsewhere.

Housing supply and demand

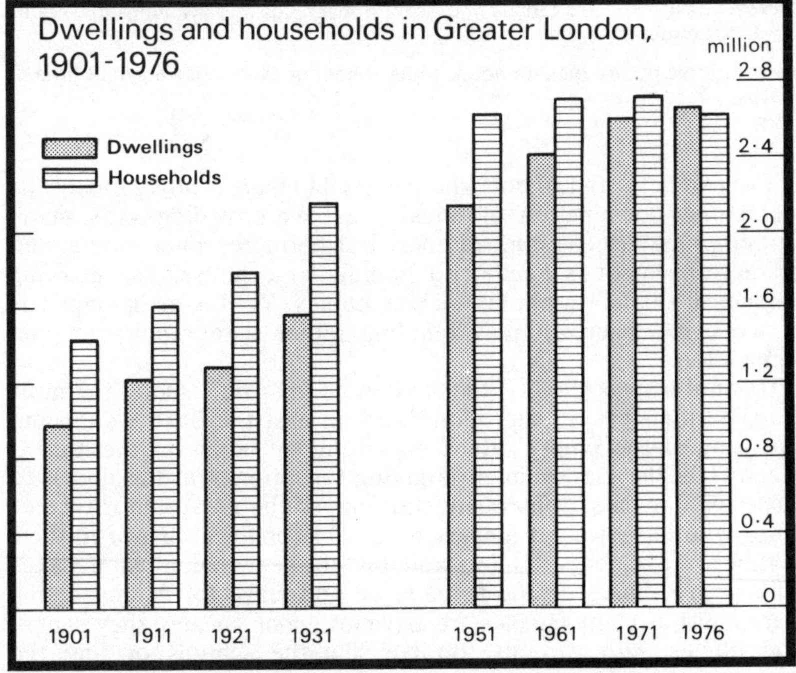

Source: Based on census data, 1976 figures on GLC estimates.

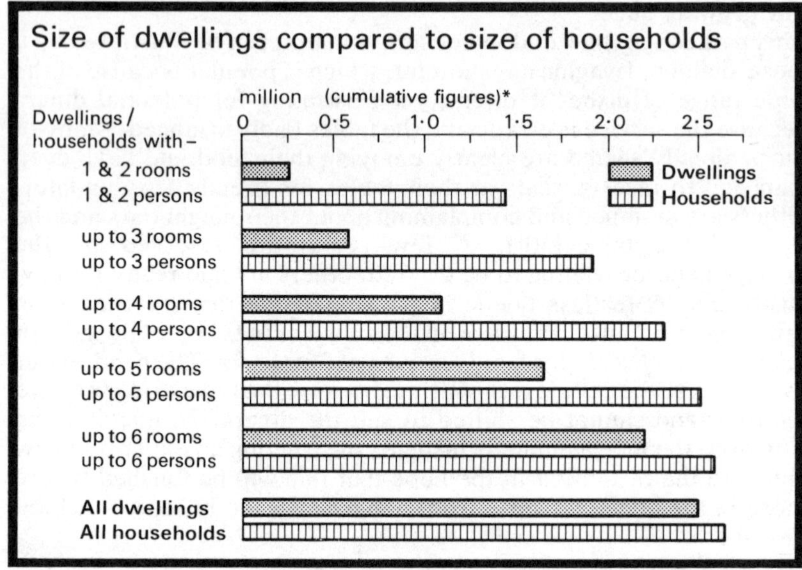

*i.e. dwellings of 'up to 3 rooms' include those with 1, 2 or 3 rooms.

Source: Based on 1971 census figures for households and dwellings in Greater London.

Note: Figures do not include households absent or dwellings vacant at time of census.

The parallel with London's housing is that there is now probably as much under-occupation of housing as overcrowding – as many half-empty tables as cramped ones. Furthermore, much conversion or rearrangement is needed to fit into large houses the growing number of small households seeking homes. Yet the main emphasis of work has been on new building rather than renovation and conversion.

It is not over-stretching the analogy to imagine some of the most hungry (homeless) at the door brushing past the head waiter and squatting at the empty tables or setting up boxes in the annex. Meanwhile the management is giving top priority in the queue to those who are most obviously starving, to the great annoyance of those who have waited longest for a table or for a change in their seating arrangements. Understandably, the general confusion makes quite a few diners decide to pack up and leave for calmer eating places, just as many families are leaving London because they cannot find homes with gardens, do not like the schools or find the environment in London unsympathetic.

To do justice to the analogy it is really necessary to picture three eating-places. One is an expensive restaurant which can only be entered with the appropriate credit card, and is equivalent to owner-occupation. Many would like to dine there, but credit (a mortgage) is not easy to come by and prices are high. The second establishment is a cafe of mixed quality with some sawdust on the floor, but some good and pricey tables, open to anyone who can tip the doorkeeper enough. This equivalent of the private rented sector has been a haven for many saving up for a blow-out elsewhere, but over the years large numbers of its tables have been taken over by the cafeteria and by the restaurant next door. The necessary tip has risen substantially. The cafeteria is the third eating place in the analogy. Most of its tables are filled, the management tries to be fair with the long queue, and the food is reasonably priced. It represents council housing where authorities have to cope both with the claims of the homeless in the queue, and with the problems of the poorly served in the cafe next door. Councils give priority on good property to those displaced by redevelopment, then the homeless and tenants wishing to transfer to another council house, and , finally, those on the waiting list.

DISTRIBUTION OF HOUSEHOLDS BY TENURE (GREATER LONDON)

	Owner occupied '000s	**Rented from local authority** '000s	**Private rented*** '000s
1961	965 36.3%	485 18.2%	1,208 45.5%
1966	1,012 38.5%	567 21.6%	1,046 39.9%
1971	1,069 40.4%	659 24.9%	921 34.7%
1976†	1,150 44.8%	725 28.3%	690 26.9%

*Includes dwellings owned by firms and leased to employees; also includes housing associations' and co-operatives' property.

†Estimated figures (based on DOE household estimates and GLC estimated distribution of dwellings by tenure).
Based on 1961, 1966 and 1971 Census data.
N.B. Figures do not include households absent at the time of Census.

No entry
A check with building societies, councils and accommodation agencies confirms the difficulties of gaining access to any of the three housing 'eating places'. A first-time purchaser in London would

usually need to earn more than £4,000 and have a deposit of £2,000 to buy a typical modest inter-war house for £13,000. Building societies are reluctant to take a wife's full income into account because she may soon give up her job. They are not enthusiastic about lending on conversions or on properties in areas of London where there is even the remotest prospect of council intervention. So although about sixty-five per cent of building society mortgages go to first-time buyers, couples need to be relatively well off to have much hope of success. Government spending cuts have severely reduced availability of council mortgages. Nor have councils been able to give much help to people wanting to rent their first home in London. Some councils will offer young married couples old property bought from landlords and in need of repair, or flats on older council estates at low rents so they can save up enough to buy a house or wait in relative comfort before claiming a higher position on the waiting list.

However, those schemes are limited and many people on the waiting list have little prospect of ever being offered a home. This is because most councils in inner London have been preoccupied in rebuilding large areas of densely packed housing, and giving first choice of new homes to those they have displaced. Council tenants wanting to move have had second choice, while there has also been mounting pressure to give priority to homeless families. In 1970, 25,000 people were housed from waiting lists; by 1975 the number had dropped to 15,000.

Privately rented accommodation is not easy to come by either. It is both scarce and expensive. In the autumn of 1976, SHAC carried out a survey of fifty accommodation agencies throughout London to find the current price of the cheapest self-contained two-room flats. The answers ranged from £20 to £80 a week, with the average £39. In at least half the flats children were not allowed, and much of the letting would be by landlords who have found loopholes in the Rent Acts that give the tenant no security from eviction. Even hostel accommodation might cost between £1 and £3 a night, bed and breakfast rather more. Humble bedsitters with shared facilities fetch £10 a week and over. The housing 'cafe' which in London has traditionally been the first stop for those setting up home, before buying a house or getting a council flat, is closing down.

Malcolm Allan of the Central London Planning Conference team has spent the past four years working on a housing plan sponsored by eight boroughs. He has become convinced that access to housing, rather than a shortage of homes or bad condition is London's main problem:

> London's housing market is in a state of organised chaos. Almost everyonc is to blame – successive national Governments, the

London boroughs, the Greater London Council, the building societies, the speculators in land and buildings, and arguing politicians. Part of the trouble is that the stock of housing is like a gangrenous body, in a state of advanced decay. The attempts to improve its condition have been successful in halting the rot, but have produced other problems. It is a story of legislation piled on legislation, and switches in policy as a result of the changing economic climate or political expediency.

Local and national governments have directed their intervention towards the private landlord, buying him out because it was there that the worst property was concentrated, and imposing successive controls to protect tenants. The landlords who remained have been faced with escalating repair and maintenance costs and saddled with the provisions of the Rent Acts that have made their business less and less profitable. Consequently, many have sold off their investments to people who wanted to buy a home. This double squeeze has dramatically reduced the amount of privately rented accommodation available. The house purchasers have been helped by tax incentives and Government manipulation of bank and building society interest rates to ensure funds are channeled into mortgage lending. Nevertheless, the rising price of homes and building society interest rates to ensure funds are channelled out of the reach of most people.

For example, the building societies have refused to lend in the decaying inner city areas because they feared that although a few people might buy homes there, councils would continue to tear down whole areas as part of their improvement policies. Since councils are now renovating rather than redeveloping in many areas, there is little excuse for continuing these restrictive policies.

Housing has been improved, whether by councils or owner-occupiers – but the process has been at the expense of those who would have spent some years in privately rented accommodation before they could afford to buy a home or or claim a council letting. These newcomers to the housing market cannot afford to buy straight away, and do not have high priority on council lists. With the demise of the private landlord they have nowhere to go.

However, as Malcolm Allan points out, it would be unfair to cast all blame upon councils and Government for concentrating on physically improving housing while failing to realise the other problems this could bring. They have been faced with appalling conditions and strong public pressure to act. After the Second World

War, London had a severe shortage of housing on the one hand and, on the other, spreading decay in the existing stock. Because most of the sites available for new housing were at that time bomb sites, policy makers tended to think in terms of large-scale, comprehensive redevelopment as the only viable way to solve London's housing shortgage.

By 1965, 483,000 new dwellings, both council and private, had been built, but the problem of the poor conditions and shortages remained. A survey carried out by the GLC in 1967 concluded that 357,000 of London's homes had a useful life of sixteen to twenty-five years, and a further 149,000 had only eight to fifteen years to go. The 120,000 with less than eight years of useful life needed to be pulled down rapidly. Borough league tables of house-building performance were published, and Housing Ministers exhorted councillors to use the high density industrialised building systems which would, in theory, quickly and cheaply clear bad housing and cut waiting lists. Much of the building involved demolition of existing houses and the aims were to overcome shortage by building more homes on the site where possible, improve conditions, and yet still leave some open spaces. All too often, the end result was costly, unattractive and in need of repair within a decade. Moreover, delays in decanting families from the sites and carrying work through offset the benefits of the extra accommodation. Inner London boroughs had to rehouse people within their own boundaries because the Green Belt and the attitudes of outer boroughs prevented building on their vacant land.

It is easy in retrospect to suggest that much of the property should have been renovated instead of redeveloped, but that was not an option open to councils at the time. Until 1974 there was no clear legislation to allow councils to use compulsory purchase powers to buy property from private landlords for renovating as opposed to redevelopment. Furthermore, Government subsidies were biased in favour of the construction of tower blocks, and building technology for renovation was less advanced than for redevelopment. The small landlords who owned most of the bad property were inevitably reluctant themselves to carry out improvements which would not be covered by the rents they could charge. Often they would have to evict their tenants before the builders could come in and, once that was achieved, selling the house for owner-occupation would be far more lucrative than reletting.

Demolition and development

In the 1950s and 1960s councils really had only two broad choices: to do very little, or to engage in a massive programme of redevelopment which would change the face of their borough and shift thousands of families around the map. Southwark was one of the councils which decided to take action. In 1965 it began a programme which will mean that by the early 1980s it will, with the GLC, own seventy per cent of the borough's homes. Southwark's council believes there may even be a surplus: the number of people in the area fell from 600,000 in 1901 to 260,000 in 1971 and could be as low as 225,000 by 1981. In a candid interview, Southwark's director of housing, John O'Brien, admitted:

> The loss of population in recent years can be largely attributed to redevelopment – there was no question of people voting with their feet, they had to go. I make no secret of the way we arrived at our building plans. When Southwark was formed from three boroughs in 1965, we put together existing slum clearance plans and decided to double the programme from 600 to 1,200 homes a year. We plotted the existing plans on a map, got into one of the council's cars and drove round the areas to see if we were wrong. We didn't change much. During the redevelopment programme the average person on the waiting list stood no chance of a council house because most were going to families displaced by redevelopment. In one year, I remember, we housed only twelve people from the list, although that has now risen to 1,300 a year and we are making substantial inroads into the waiting list.

However, Mr. O'Brien claims that when they have completed their programme in the early 1980s, with the expected surplus of housing, they will open their doors to virtually anyone. The old estates and many of the tower blocks will be let to students and young people for a few pounds a week. Council tenants will be allowed to have spare rooms, so that a couple will be able to raise a family without moving. Without its massive housing programme and its displacement of so many people from the borough, Southwark maintains it would not be in this position. It is the one borough which has produced a written housing strategy, and is now switching to renovation of property. Some newly built estates are most attractive.

But changes take a long time to accomplish and at the moment many of Southwark's residents are discontented. In a survey carried out by the council, fifty-nine per cent of those questioned said that they would like to be owner-occupiers; only fourteen per cent actually are. They longed for houses with gardens, trees and quiet streets rather than the soulless slabs built by the council in the 1960s and early 1970s. But very few of Southwark's families earn enough to buy a house. Under present housing finance arrangements they have no alternative but council housing. Interestingly, the survey also revealed that more than half the people who were living in conditions officially classified as very poor, actually thought them not too bad. This finding casts some doubt on the use of official criteria used to measure bad repair and lack of amenities. It may be that some people

HOUSING STRESS AND STABILITY

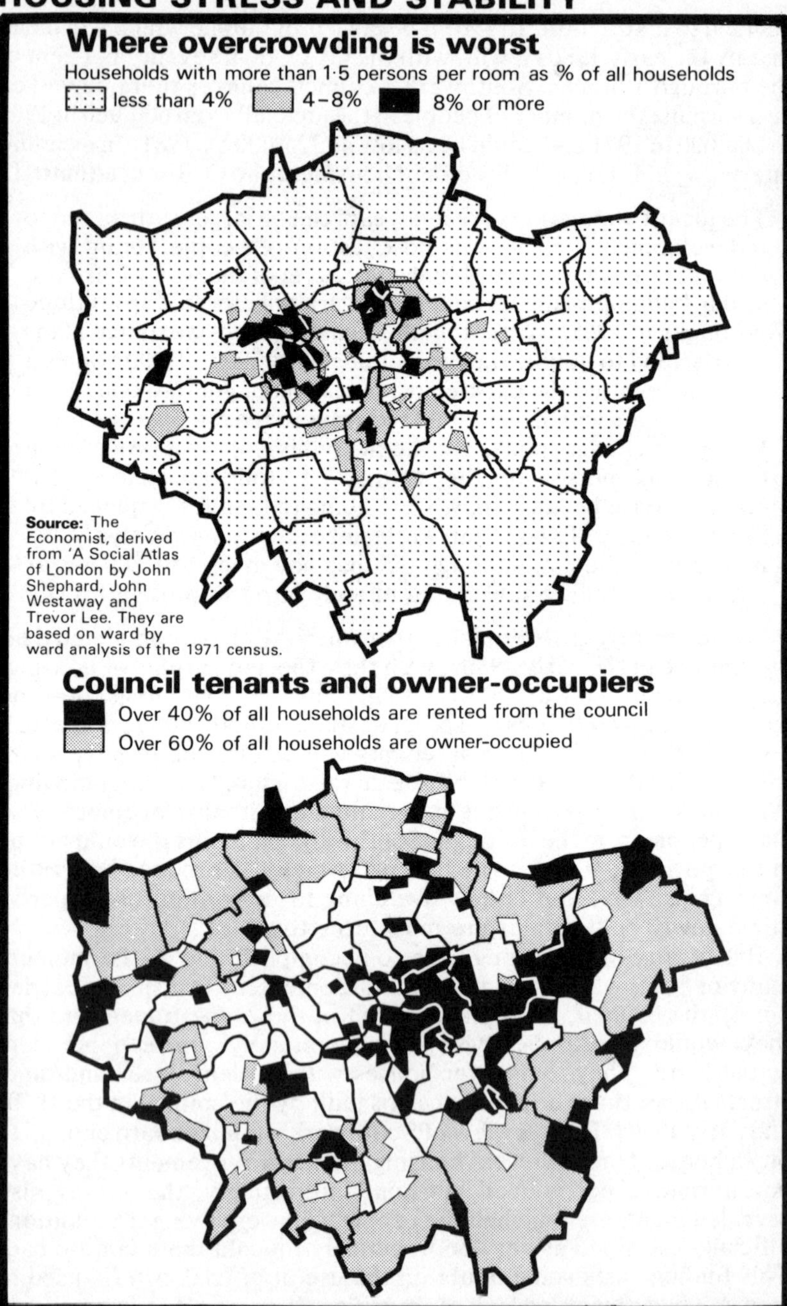

are prepared to put up with an outside lavatory for the sake of a low rent; or that many are elderly and have got used to the inconvenience. Even if some people are content with sub-standard housing, most expect better and better housing. New homes should last at least sixty years and satisfy their tenants during that time. The results of building cheaply in the 1930s are everywhere to see: families on the waiting list refuse to accept flats only thirty to forty years old.

Southwark and many other councils have taken the view that high quality council housing should be provided at relatively low cost to the tenant. So long as there was a fairly obvious housing shortage in London, councils felt justified in building at whatever the price, particularly since Government subsidised most of the initial costs. Camden, which has been attacked most strongly for building costly homes, has spent up to £54,000 a home in a few instances. Since the cost for councils of borrowing money has increased, while rents have been held down, subsidies have soared.

In a confidential report prepared for the Department of the Environment and leaked in August 1976 by the *Sunday Times,* Alex Henney suggested that with a crude balance of homes and families in prospect, the building of unduly expensive council houses could no longer be justified. In terms of the restaurant analogy, more resources should go into shifting the tables and improving the quality of service than in building the annex. 'I do not specify precisely the meaning of unduly expensive, but like an elephant, one knows it when one sees it,' wrote Mr Henney. When professional fees and interest charges were added to the land and building costs, he maintained, the average costs of building a council home in inner London, outer London and the edge of London were in 1975 respectively £27,500, £20,500 and £15,000. He recommended that where building in inner London was unduly expensive, it should be cut as soon as possible, and that further council housing should be concentrated in outer London where it would both be cheaper and allow poorer people to escape from inner London.

Mr Henney's suggestions reinforced recommendations made in a succession of official reports since Milner Holland's in 1965 that overcrowding in inner London can be eased by building new council estates in outer London; or, in those suburbs where there are relatively short waiting lists, by allocating some of the vacancies to inner London families. Most outer London boroughs have instead used their planning powers wherever possible to stop any 'invasion' by inner boroughs or the GLC.

The housing strategy

When Labour took control of the GLC in 1973, the housing development chairman, Gladys Dimson, did attempt to establish for the first time a London-wide strategy which would improve conditions in the private rented sector and coerce outer London into helping inner London. The aim was for the GLC to step in where boroughs were not pulling their weight. The strategy advocated buying out private landlords so their property could be improved, building more in outer London, and ensuring that all councils shared the burdens of those with the longest waiting lists. Mrs Dimson's policy of 'municipalisation' was pursued with great enthusiasm until the GLC decided to cut spending and Mrs Dimson was replaced as chairman by Richard Balfe. In three years, some 6,500 homes were bought by the GLC and an estimated 19,000 by the boroughs. There were problems: the housing department could not improve property as quickly as it was being bought.

Other aspects of the strategy also ran into difficulties. The housing targets plan – by which each borough would have to ensure that if private developers were not putting up homes, they should do so themselves – remained a paper exercise because there was nobody to crack the whip if any borough refused to co-operate. The GLC has limited powers and not always the political will, while the Government remains on the sidelines. Nor did the common allocation system survive Labour's term in County Hall. The idea was that all boroughs would make available, from the council homes they owned, a common pool of housing which could go to those in greatest need, wherever they lived. The boroughs could not reach agreement, basically because most of them took the parochial if understandable view that they had to look after their own. Tony Judge, chairman of the GLC's housing management committee, is quite explicit on why boroughs will not cooperate.

> I always suspected that however desirable a common allocation policy was, we would not achieve it because of the crazy set-up of a split in powers between boroughs and the GLC. In terms of local politics, councils were not prepared to help each other. And I think, quite bluntly, that race enters into it. The saddest remark was made by the leader of one outer borough, controlled not by the Tories but by Labour. He said that he wasn't going to have the dross of inner London in his borough. For dross read black. Some of the outer boroughs, Labour as well as Tory, are concerned about a wave of nominations of tenants from inner London because that is where there is a concentration of under-privileged blacks. We now have a very expensive nomination system by which we work out agreements with outer London boroughs. But when you realise that the fourteen outer London boroughs between them hardly house ten families a week from inner London, you realise how pathetic the whole thing is.

Mr Judge's frank exposition of the reality of housing politics should, however, be tempered by consideration of the attempt he and Richard Balfe made to establish with the boroughs a framework for London housing policy. In January 1977, the GLC produced broad guidelines for action in housing over the next decade. The report, *Housing Policies and Programme,* points out that by the mid-1980s about 56,000 homes will have to be demolished because they are either beyond repair or stand in areas needed for parks, roads and other schemes. This rate of demolition will be only about one third of that reached in the peak year of 1969. Besides the demolitions, 383,000 homes are estimated to be in need of improvements ranging from a new bathroom to total renovation. On this basis, some new building and a major renovation programme is needed.

Some agreements have been reached with boroughs in talks following the earlier GLC strategy. There is a consensus that over 9,000 acres of land for housing could be available in London during the next decade, and there is some prospect that limited agreement will be reached on a London-wide allocation system for council housing, so that the chance of getting a home is less dependent upon where a family is living at the time than its degree of need for a better home.

Inevitably, the 1977 strategy is politically contentious. It proposes that the municipalisation programme of buying out private landlords should continue at 850 to 1,000 homes a year, and that new council housing should be concentrated in outer London where there is more space. Like Mrs Dimson's strategy, it has the virtue of trying to provide some overall framework for fitting homes to households and improving conditions. However, reasoned official documents are not always the basis for housing policy. When the pressure is on, the complexities are forgotten and the one-shot solutions pressed into service. During the GLC election campaign of 1977, voters have been bombarded with the usual party statements, the promises and panaceas. Both parties promised to tackle the worsening problem of access to housing for those without a home, while not upsetting the majority of voters.

You can't please everyone . . .

This is the heart of the matter. Most of the problems in housing are at the margin – they are about those who are being thrown out of homes, cannot get into the housing system, or need better homes. The majority of people are well housed, and subsidies, tax relief and rent controls have often meant they get more and better housing than they might otherwise afford. So while there is no shortage – in the crude sense that there is a balance of homes and households – the distribution of housing is inequitable. Those on the outside trying to get in can only be helped if those already well housed move around and make more room – or if still more homes are built and the balance moves into a housing surplus situation. Even this costly over-supply policy will not work unless the extra space created goes to those on the margin instead of being snapped up by others able to buy spare rooms, and commuters seeking to live nearer the centre.

HOUSING COSTS IN LONDON

	Council rents	**Private rents**	**Mortgage payments**	**Average house prices**	**Household income**	**Retail Price Index**
	p.w. £	*p.w. £*	*p.w. £*	*£*	*p.w. £*	*Jan'74=100*
	1	*2*	*3*	*4*	*5*	*6*
1970	3.12	5.67	8.88	6,882	40.52	73.1
	100.0	*100.0*	*100.0*	*100.0*	*100.0*	*100.0*
1971	3.43	6.19	10.31	7,837	43.85	80.0
	110	*109.2*	*116.1*	*113.9*	*108.2*	*109.4*
1972	3.82	6.63	13.44	11,113	50.67	85.7
	122.4	*116.9*	*151.4*	*161.5*	*125.1*	*117.2*
1973	4.15	6.61	17.48	14,447	56.54	93.5
	133.0	*116.6*	*196.9*	*209.9*	*139.5*	*127.9*
1974	4.37	7.60	19.50	14,857	61.10	108.5
	140.0	*134.0*	*219.6*	*215.9*	*150.8*	*148.4*
1975	4.65	7.67	21.44	14,918	83.21	134.8
	149.0	*135.3*	*241.4*	*216.8*	*205.4*	*184.4*
1976	5.05	8.08	23.23	15,649		157.1
	161.9	*142.5*	*261.6*	*227.4*		*214.9*

Figures in italics are indices with 1970 equals 100 in each column.

Notes:

1. Council rents given are average for the year and for 1976 April only.
2. Private rents given are the fair rents per tenancy for unfurnished accommodation determined under the Housing Acts of 1965/68 and do not represent the market rents; first half of 1976 only.
3. Based on data from the Building Societies Mortgages Survey 1976 3rd quarter.
4. Based on data from the Building Societies Mortgages Survey: 1976 3rd quarter; figures given represent gross payments; see page 95 for further explanation.
5. Households income: gross income from the Family Expenditure Survey, 1976 not available.
6. Retail price index, average of 12 months.

The point is well illustrated by the impossibility of helping both existing owner-occupiers, who form the majority of the voters, and those who want to buy homes, about whom politicians are also concerned. Owners want their mortgage payments to be kept down, their house values up, and their ability to move unfettered; while potential buyers want to get mortgages easily and to have plenty of houses on offer. Keeping payments down means keeping interest rates low. This tends to dry up the building societies' funds because savers put their money where there are higher rates of return. Low interest rates therefore mean fewer mortgages, which is not much consolation for potential borrowers. Yet if the politician tries to help these borrowers with high interest rates and easy lending, and perhaps giving grants to cover the costs of deposits, there may be an explosion of house prices as more and more people chase the limited number of homes for sale. This helps no one except the house owner who wants to sell out and live in a tent. If he wants to move to another house he has to join in the costly chase like everyone else. All that happens is that house buying is driven further up-market.

The only way to encourage owner-occupation in reality is to increase the number of houses on the market. However, building new homes for sale each year in London adds less than one per cent to the available stock; the house-buying market is almost entirely second-hand. The other solution therefore is to take homes from the other sectors or, in terms of the original analogy, annex some tables from the cafe and cafeteria. This means selling council houses or buying from private landlords. The latter is the main process by which owner-occupation has grown in London by an estimated 10.5 per cent between 1971 and 1976.

Each of these courses of action presents problems. Most council tenants cannot afford to buy their homes, even with a substantial discount, and if council housing is sold it is generally the better houses with gardens which go, not the flats which make up much of inner London municipal property. Building societies are reluctant to lend on council houses, so the local authority has to lend the tenant the money. Much of the financial advantage to the council is thus lost. If there are fewer council homes because some have been sold, less become available for re-letting as tenants move or die, allowing fewer offers to be made to those on the waiting list. If all the best property is sold off, then the council is left with a poor range of homes to offer. On the other hand, if house hunters are encouraged to buy out private landlords, those wishing to rent will find it more and more difficult to do so. Any promises to improve dramatically the ability of people to become owner-occupiers should therefore be treated with scepticism.

Scepticism should similarly be applied to political prescriptions for the private rented sector, whether they aim to keep landlords in operation or provide alternatives. For the Tories, Margaret Thatcher favours allowing landlords to let under a new 'shorthold' form of lease by which the landlord could regain possession should he want to stop letting any of the property. The aim is to encourage the landlord to stay in business. Rents would be fixed by the rent officers or, in a shortage situation, by agreement with the tenant. Critics suggest that if they could get rid of their tenants so easily, landlords would simply sell out when the market was best, thus reducing the private rented sector still further. The real problem is that private renting is not a commercial proposition at the sorts of rents most people can afford. Subsidies in the form of tax relief to owner-occupiers, together with past housing shortages, have kept house prices up. However, the landlord cannot make a profit because of tax on rents, higher interest rates, and repair costs. So while rent controls have helped make letting unattractive, they have also, paradoxically, forced landlords to stay in business – without security for tenants, more landlords would have sold out. Many are locked into an unprofitable position and consequently make little effort to improve the property.

Labour proposes a different release, suggesting that the private landlord should be replaced by the local authority, in the belief that this in itself is a change for the better. There may indeed be more prospect of repairs, and concern for the tenant, but this crude form of municipalisation ignores the very different functions that the private and public landlords fulfil. The one advantage of the private landlord is that he does not expect home hunters to have spent five years living in London, and perhaps two years in the borough, before putting them on a waiting list. His main test is how much the customer will pay. This is, of course, little consolation to a family with two children competing against four secretaries for a flat with a rent of £40 a week. But it does ensure that London firms can recruit secretaries instead of having to move out of London or press the Government to subsidise commuter fares. The problems and abuses in the private rented sector were well catalogued by Milner Holland's report. But even he warned strongly against cutting the number of private landlords, and the Francis Committee report of 1971 recommended against the security of tenure for furnished tenants, granted in 1974, precisely because this would seize up the system.

Without the private landlord, whatever his failings, the housing log-jam could get worse, not better. Boroughs such as Southwark, which maintain they will soon have a housing surplus and so will be able to let council property without the current restrictions, are not necessarily being realistic. Surpluses only arise when there is more supply than demand and, so long as London has a fairly buoyant job market, people will want to live in or near the capital. At present people decide where to live by balancing the time and cost of travelling with the cost and desirability of the accommodation they can get. If inner London boroughs suddenly say they have got homes to spare, some people will wish to move further into the centre to cut their travelling time and costs. Unless councils start to charge the highest possible rents for their property, in effect behaving like a private landlord, they will end up with another waiting list of a different sort.

Tangled finances

Council housing, owner-occupation and private renting must be seen as complementary rather than competing sectors. Each is needed, and care must be exercised in cutting or expanding any sector at the expense of another. Private renting is essential to allow newcomers and those setting up home to squeeze into the housing system, to accommodate visitors and to allow people to move around without the great costs of buying or selling and the difficulties of transfer from council property. Owner-occupation provides security, choice and a ladder to better accommodation. But council housing is the only hope of good accommodation for a high proportion of Londoners. It has the great benefit that although new property is heavily subsidised, the older property can yield 'profits' to the council because rents have gone up and more than cover the councils' costs of borrowing. For this reason, it is highly misleading to compare the first-year costs of home ownership with first-year costs of a new council house. The direct comparison is convenient for the Tories, because it shows a high subsidy to the council tenant to cover the difference between rent and council outgoings, and a lower initial subsidy through tax relief to an owner-occupier.

But provided council management and repair costs are kept in hand, the position changes dramatically after ten or fifteen years. By then the council house may well be yielding a profit as rents have gone up with inflation, while one of two things will have happened to the owner-occupier. Either he will be making relatively low mortgage payments (perhaps no more than council rents) and sitting on a substantial asset. Or he will have moved once or twice to better property, collecting bigger subsidies on the way because the higher payments attract higher tax relief. Switching from council housing to owner-occupation does not in itself cut subsidies for a government; what is gained in lower subsidies to council tenants may be lost in tax foregone by the Chancellor when the tenants become owners.

So far, successive Governments have not concerned themselves with trying to establish which form of tenure is best suited to particular people and areas. Instead, rents have been held down and subsidies increased, mortgage tax relief maintained at high levels. Policy has been directed towards helping those already in housing, rather than those trying to gain entry. The result is that councils have had to cut housing programmes because so much is being spent in subsidies, and owner-occupiers are encouraged to consume more and more space. The tangle has become almost impossible to unravel because owner-occupiers and council tenants rely on tax relief and subsidies to maintain their standards of living in the face of higher and higher direct taxation. Yet unless the Environment Secretary and the Chancellor agree to sort out housing finance, the housing 'haves' will continue to keep out the 'have nots'.

Suggested reading

Milner Holland report on housing in Greater London (HMSO Cmnd 2605 1965)
Francis report on the Rent Acts (HMSO Cmnd 4609 1971)
Homelessness in London, John Greve, Dyllis Page, Stella Greve (Scottish Academic Press 1971)
Housing Strategy Plan (GLC 1974)
Housing Review Panel Report (Camden 1976)
Housing Strategy (Southwark 1977)
The Organisation of Housing, M. Harloe, R. Issacharoff, R. Minns (Heinemann 1974)
Guide to Housing (Housing Centre Trust 1977)
The Government of Housing, D. V. Donnison (Pelican 1967)
Housing Policy and the Housing System, A. Murie, P. Niner, C. Watson (Allen and Unwin 1976)

THE THREE-RING CITY

CENTRAL LONDON

Many of the rows about the future of London which have been given prominence in the media over the past few years have appeared to be about the environment of central London. The roll call of concern has swept around Westminster and Camden, Kensington and Chelsea: the rebuilding of Trafalgar Square and Piccadilly Circus, the preservation of village-like Covent Garden, the retention of tailoring shops in Soho, the renovation of Tolmers Square, the curtailing of embassies and hotels around Cromwell Road and Queen's Gate. Often the conflicts have been presented in terms of developers and planners versus residents; victory judged on whether a building stays up or is demolished.

The change in London's face has been real enough, although perhaps it has not always been for the worse. The pyramidal tumble of carefully detailed glass, granite and stainless steel boxes, designed by Elsom, Pack and Roberts to replace the late-nineteenth-century buildings of Victoria Street, has been welcomed by many as one of the most aesthetically exciting office schemes in central London for years. Are the buildings in Trafalgar Square either side of Northumberland Avenue so fine that they could not be bettered by modern replacements which would have the bonus of improved working conditions? And does it make sense to preserve Covent Garden as a base for local craft industries when the Fleet Line tube is being extended nearby to the Strand as a better commuter route? Some buildings, bought by councils when the market moved to Nine Elms in Battersea, could be renovated or redeveloped as offices; this would considerably benefit ratepayers, instead of mainly providing subsidised accommodation for groups which might well find a home not far away, but in premises for which they could afford to pay a reasonable rent.

The point is that arguments which appear to be about the changing face of central London are really about far more organic

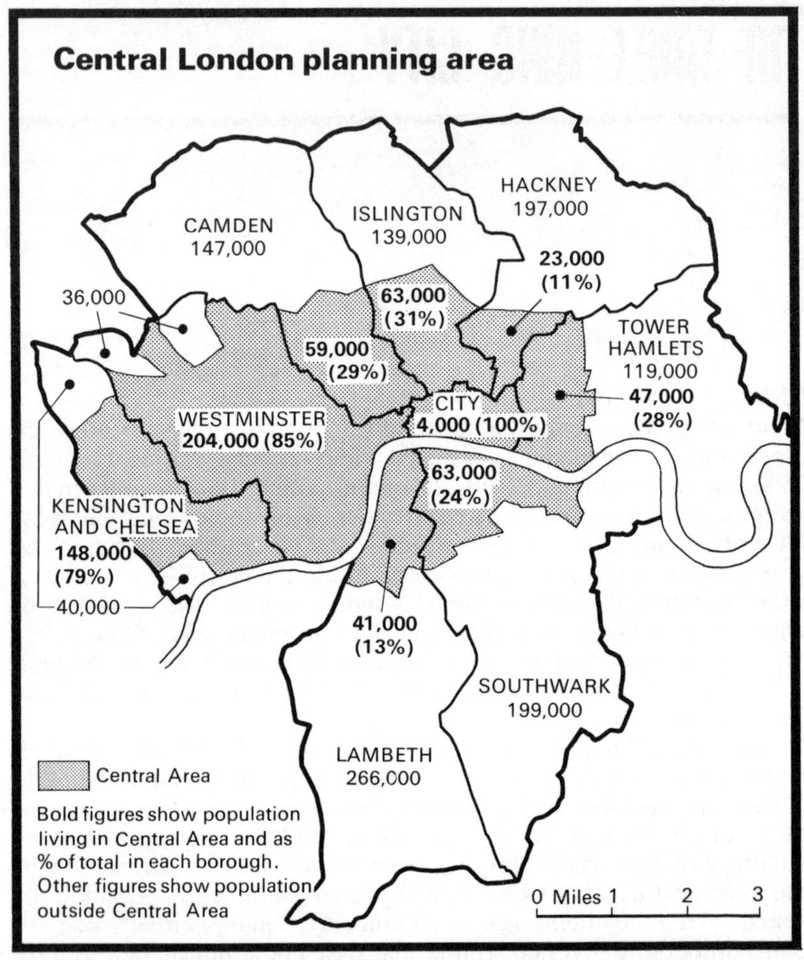

Source: Adapted from *The Advisory Plan for Central London,* 1976 based on 1971 census, small area (ward) statistics.

transformations. There is pressure to change the buildings because London itself is evolving. It is changing the way in which it makes its money and, therefore, the sort of residents it attracts and the workers it needs to service its changing population and economy. The conflict is particularly intense at the centre because so many activities, old and new, are struggling for a foothold.

There are certain traditional activities that thrive in the centre simply because London is a capital city. National institutions of Government, the Monarchy, the City, the Law Courts, the British

Museum, the National Gallery, all are housed there. And around these institutions gather journalists and solicitors, employers' organisations, foreign embassies, lobbyists, which feed off them. These traditional capital city activities, which will surely stay in London, also generate their own attraction for tourists who flock in to view the historic, physical envelopes of power and to enjoy the cultural life associated with them.

Other activities, which were thriving forty years ago but have not depended so directly upon the capital's traditional activities, have largely disappeared because they now operate better elsewhere and because other users who can pay higher rents, are pressing to take the space. Industry has moved from old multi-storey workshops to single-storey modern factories away from the centre, leaving behind shells which can be taken over by silversmiths or glass-blowers, watchmakers or other craftsmen whose skills are in demand; or by architects and publishers, small magazines and consultants who want to be in the centre but cannot afford West End premises. The West End itself is changing: the old rag trade workshops are under pressure because landlords know they can get a higher rent if the building is converted to a small film or recording studio, for example.

The demand for space changes year by year as business operations alter. Firms find that high rents and rates make it more sensible to move clerical operations to the suburbs, where rents and rates are lower, retaining a smart headquarters only for senior executives. Foreign banks want a branch in the City. In each case the Victorian warren which housed clerks is unlikely to be suitable: it must be rebuilt or renovated.

Politicians and planners have the whip-hand because they can, and do, prevent some changes and encourage others. Without planning regulations, space would go to whoever could pay the highest rents; the corner shops, workshops and offices for small professional firms would be forced out. To protect the weaker but essential businesses against the market forces of the strong, planners zone areas for industry, offices, housing. The trouble is that plans drawn up in the 1950s have not always been altered. Zones marked down for industry have not been allowed to change function as firms moved out: offices have been refused permission because they do not conform to a vision of the capital which is twenty years out of date. The result is that in some zones there is no activity at all. For years, the planners of Islington and, until recently, Tower Hamlets have opposed any spread of offices into areas such as Clerkenwell and Spitalfields in case it meant that light industry would be displaced, workers made redundant, and only developers would profit. In the event, the industry has moved out or closed down, leaving dereliction.

In central London, planners should be especially wary of imposing rigid controls; the congestion that already exists there, together with the continuing demand for space, make it essential to maximise use of the area. This is not to deny the need to protect the thousands of important buildings and preserve areas of special quality, but a balance must be struck between the many competing interests. There is no benefit in retaining out-dated restrictions which reduce the scope for change where it does least harm.

Welcome visitors

The demand for change and the potential benefits it can offer to London are illustrated by tourism, both business and leisure. This is one area in which, provided we can accommodate the visitors, London stands to make an increasing amount of money. The foreign businessman is estimated to spend an average of £45 to £60 a day in London, on his hotel, shopping, drinks, entertainment and tube travel. Without business visitors and sight-seeing tourists the theatres and hotels, Oxford Street and Knightsbridge would all look pretty sickly.

NUMBER OF VISITORS TO SELECTED TOURIST ATTRACTIONS IN CENTRAL LONDON ('000s)

	1969	**1970**	**1971**	**1972**	**1973**	**1974**	**1975**
St Paul's Cathedral	—	—	3,000	4,000	2,500	3,500	3,500
British Museum	2,000	2,300	2,695	2,761	2,318	2,101	3,313
Tower of London	2,278	2,498	2,661	2,883	2,810	2,394	2,586
Natural History Museum	1,368	1,489	1,510	1,517	1,876	1,700	2,503
Science Museum	—	—	—	1,936	2,312	2,052	2,278
National Gallery	1,553	1,750	1,859	1,774	1,616	1,629	2,038
Madame Tussauds	1,500	1,700	1,700	1,900	1,900	1,800	1,900
Jewel House	—	1,695	1,822	1,867	1.748	1,034	1,868
London Zoo	1,875	1,794	1,942	1,977	2,045	1,958	1,800

Source: London Tourist Board Annual Report 1976.

Geoffrey Smith, who runs the London Convention Bureau, says: Suddenly, this year, the business has caught up with the availability: one Government forecast estimates that as many as 80,000 more beds in the medium price range will be needed by 1980. London has been given a big boost by the new conference centre opened at Wembley, and will benefit when the Barbican centre opens in two years. A big conference – for instance the American Bar Association – brings about 10,000 people here. It could be worth between three and four million pounds to London, so is obviously well worth promoting.

In November, we're bringing one of our most interesting success stories here – an organisation with 30,000 members called the Sweet Adelines, American ladies who sing in barber shop quartets. It took us four years to talk to them and get to know them. We went to their meetings all over America – Seattle, Washington, Milwaukee – then got the Ambassador in Washington to give a party at the Embassy for their board. He spoke very nicely about London, acted as a salesman. Illtyd Harrington came over with us in the following year and made a speech rather like Dylan Thomas or Lloyd George which went down awfully well; so they're coming. 6,000 of them will be here next year. They're mostly housewives, but that will probably be worth a couple of million pounds to London. So its worth the GLC's while to sponsor us to do that sort of thing.

Most of our meetings are less dramatic – about one or two hundred people. But altogether we think this business is worth about sixty million pounds each year and we think its growing by about ten per cent a year. Conferences are a growth market. Nowadays, people with problems want to get together and have meetings to discuss them. What we're concerned about is that they should hold their meetings in London.

In 1977, tourism generally is expected to bring over £2,000 million into the country, much of it coming into London. The number of overseas visitors to the capital is expected to rise from 7.5 million in 1976 to 8.6 million in Jubilee year, and increase by ten per cent annually thereafter. The hotel industry, encouraged by a government grant of £1,000 per bedroom, invested about £200 million in creating more bedspaces in the late 1960s and early 1970s and for a few years there was a surplus. The slack has now been taken up by tourists prepared to pay £10 – £15 a night, and the London Tourist Board says there is a shortage of more reasonably priced beds for people on package tours. At present, no new hotels are being started. John Bosman, group consultant to EMI's hotels and restaurant division, maintains there will continue to be a big demand for hotel beds, yet few hotels will be built:

The cost of building hotels in London is so high today that I find it difficult to believe that private enterprise is going to produce the capital to do it. I don't think there'll ever be any more Government grants. I think we are going to be faced with overcrowding in the next five years. What we've got to do is as they've done in America – have a cheaper range of hotels, a cheaper form of service: self catering, and hotels on the perimeter where people can stay economically. The luxury hotel as we know it, the five star hotel, will no longer be built. I think the Intercontinental at Hyde Park Corner is probably the last one that will go up in London. Not that they're not doing extremely good business – they are. But to build a hotel like the Intercontinental today would cost about £45,000 a bedroom. That's not a businessman's proposition and not where the great new market is going to be: the great movement is going to be with the middle classes of the world, not with a few film stars and Arab potentates. Go to Heathrow today and look at the sort of people who are travelling – people who never thought of moving out of their homesteads twenty years ago, but who now think nothing of flying thousands of miles. They're the ones we have to provide for, they're the ones who can bring us commercial success. It's in the package tours that we really have to look for the future money.

John Bosman thinks that not only will hotels have to adapt, but so will popular catering:

You can classify the restaurant business into three sections. There are luxury gastronomic restaurants, which attract the wealthy tourist or businessman; then you get the huge range of middle-class restaurants, the mum and dad restaurants, bistros; then you get the popular restaurants or cafes such as the Golden Egg. The real growth area is in the popular catering. We've just seen McDonalds come to England with their high technology and expertise. I am of the opinion that they will sweep the country. They have a form of very moderate eating, what I describe as the finger-eating, table-clearing concept, which the British public are now beginning to accept. The product is extremely good and the technology is superb. I don't think a British public is now beginning to accept. The product is technology to do it. It sounds ridiculous: what goes into producing a hamburger and a bun? But you go there and you'll be back. I don't know why. But it has a different system. Children love it. I think that many British firms are considering at the moment whether they can climb on to that bandwagon. It's going to make a very big impression on the eating habits of this country.

The benefits of tourism naturally seem rather illusory to Londoners jostled from their native pavements by foreign crowds each summer. Travellers on the Circle line, and Oxford Street shoppers may feel that the extra congestion and the tiresome task of giving directions are high prices to pay for foreign currency. The South Kensington resident who has to suffer large coach parties arriving and departing for the airport at highly unsociable hours may be forgiven a lack of concern for the balance of payments. Yet without the tourists, central London would suffer far more distressing changes than their arrival has caused. Theatres and restaurants would close by the score, large numbers of hotel staff would be unemployed. Whether we like it or not, we are saddled with tourists, conferences and change. At least, if we discourage them, we will have to put up with a lower standard of living, and a less entertaining London.

Sir Donald Albery, chairman of Wyndham Theatres Ltd., which takes a detailed census of customers every month, estimates that well over a third of his theatres' seats are filled by foreign bottoms:

> Fifty per cent of all tourists who come to London come in order to go to the theatre. This is a low figure for English-speaking tourists. All enquiries made by the BTA have indicated very clearly that of all the things that they pay for, the theatre is their first priority. They say they have come for the countryside, the galleries, museums and general sightseeing (which are all free), and the theatre.
>
> We talk of the value of exports, or invisible earnings; but what export is there of such pure quality as a theatre ticket? If we sell, say, ten million pounds-worth of exported cars, that doesn't mean we've made that amount of profit, because we've had to import an immense amount of materials in order to make those cars. Whereas the only thing the tourist who buys a theatre ticket takes away is a tiny bit of paper. Therefore it is a very pure export and probably every million pounds spent in the theatre in a year is worth a lot more than almost any other million pounds of export business that you can think of. A hotel manager said to me not long ago, 'the theatre is London's all-the-year-round sunshine'. In the future I think we in the theatre are going to depend on the tourist completely.

Room for expansion

Additional tourists will present accommodation problems. So will the continuing demand for offices. There are relatively few empty modern offices in London at the moment, and once the economy revives there will be pressure for new ones to be built. This will produce a conflict between the desire to protect areas of Kensington, Westminster and the City from change, and the need to provide firms with premises near enough to existing offices for senior staff to enjoy the advantages of face to face meetings without an hour's journey each way.

The Advisory Plan for Central London, drawn up by a team of planners working for eight boroughs, identifies several 'soft' areas where changes in activity or physical structure could most easily be accommodated. The north bank of the Thames is one such area. The City Corporation is already building new roads, schools and offices, and south-west of St Paul's there is further scope for limited change.

Across the Thames in Lambeth and Southwark there is even more potential. Former plans for building a 'city within a city' along Hays Wharf foundered because of planning delays and the collapse of the property market; but in the long term there may still be the opportunity to build a mixture of offices, flats and entertainment which would be much more in keeping with central Londoners' needs than current plans further west. There, along the south bank, the GLC and Lambeth council have agreed to a scheme for low density housing and factories. Although this is what local people said they wanted, the decision may well turn out to have cost the councils (and the ratepayers) millions of pounds in lost rates on offices and rents on flats. The housing will be expensive and the factories may not even materialise.

Similarly, Finsbury, just north of the City, would be an ideal location for offices, but Islington still hopes to attract back industry. The acres of unused land are therefore more likely to remain derelict than be developed. The areas around stations have potential for redevelopment: British Rail hopes to redevelop Victoria Station, as well as Liverpool Street, and there is some potential around King's Cross. In the longer term there might be plans for Paddington and Marylebone Stations, if these schemes could retain most historic buildings on the sites.

The danger is that if permission for redevelopment is refused in these soft areas, pressure will build up at points where it could do worse damage to central London's diverse character. The change may come not by the obvious process of demolition and rebuilding, but by the displacement of small businesses by large. The much publicised threat to publishers and trades linked to theatres in Covent Garden is one example: the community association may have fought off proposals for major development only to find that rent reviews prove just as much a threat. As leases fall in, firms will be pushed out by higher rents as surely as if the demolition gangs had moved in. If there is a shortage of accommodation, the strong will push out the weak just as surely in commercial property as in residential: indeed, more easily because the legislation gives less security.

Rooms to let

In housing, the process of change in central London is well under way. Single people and couples can afford, per person, to pay a higher rent than a family. Many are secretaries, students, bank clerks, computer programmers, sharing bedsitters and flats in Earls Court and Queensway, Paddington and Pimlico, and their way of life changes the areas in which they live. Bedsitters cost £10 a week or more, the streets are not always particularly clean, and there is a fair chance of being kept awake at weekends by the party next door. The

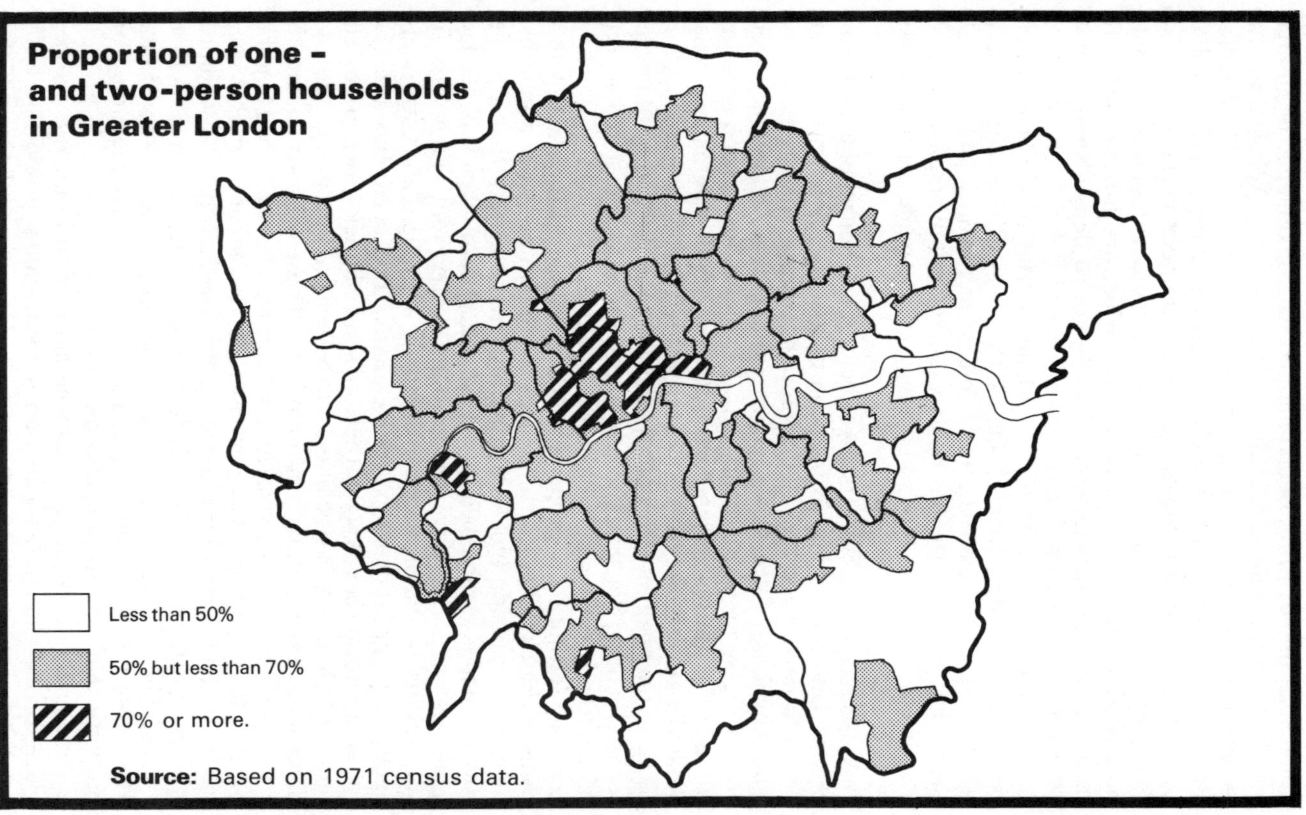
Proportion of one -
and two-person households
in Greater London
Less than 50%
50% but less than 70%
70% or more.
Source: Based on 1971 census data.

compensation lies in the social life and the convenience of all-night supermarkets, kebab restaurants and launderettes. Whole areas are being taken over by the young and single, and abandoned by families. Projections carried out by the GLC suggest that by 1981 there will be up to thirty per cent fewer families in the four central boroughs than ten years before. Families need space, nursery centres, schools, parks and safe streets — all the facilities which are difficult and costly to provide in central London. This is not to deny that it is quite possible to bring up a family in the heart of Soho — and plenty of tailors have, living over their workshops. But it would be rather perverse of planners to work against the trend. If the young want to live close-packed near the centre, and can pay to do so, why not help them? Theoretically there is no impediment, but in practise there is a steady erosion of the type of housing that has made central London what it is.

At the moment, about sixty per cent of the households rent from private landlords, some in mansion blocks complete with lifts and porter, others in overcrowded Victorian terraces, sharing bathrooms and kitchens. Successive governments have maintained rent controls, given tenants security from eviction, introduced penalties to curb the abuses of landlords. But the result now is that small landlords are often keen to sell out to councils or housing associations because they cannot carry out the repairs required and would rather realise their capital than risk the uncertain returns dictated by rent officers and tribunals. Even large landlords like Freshwater have given up letting their property and are selling off the flats in their mansion blocks. The consequences for the property are admirable: owners of mansion block flats are anxious to ensure that a proper sinking fund is established to pay for a new roof when it is needed. Councils and housing associations carry out high-standard conversions on old property, installing new kitchens and bathrooms, central heating and damp-proof courses. The occupants are also fortunate, for if they bought, they did so at a knock-down price. The rents of housing associations and council property are not unreasonable, particularly after rebate. Those who suffer are the young professionals who would, ten years ago, have clubbed together to rent a flat from Freshwater or Key Flats, Berger or Stern Holdings; or the students and young couples who now find that the landlords who do stay in business let only to foreigners who are more likely to vacate. There is little point going to the housing associations: most have closed their waiting lists and are only re-housing tenants from property they buy from landlords.

An equally important issue is whether central London is the best place for the elderly, who also form a substantial proportion of the small households. Often they are living in accommodation which is much larger than they need once their children have left home. As a result there is now more under-occupation of housing in central London than overcrowding. This is a difficult problem to solve. Moving house is a major upheaval, and few elderly people want the problems of letting off rooms. Councils have had some success in offering to buy under-occupied property and rehouse the elderly, but this has so far made little impact.

Room for manoeuvre

There is one success story for the planners in central London: traffic. Residents suffering heavy lorries pounding through their streets at night, or unable to find a parking space outside their house might not agree, but at least buses and taxis, cars and lorries are moving as fast as they were ten years ago. The computerised traffic lights, one-way systems and parking controls have enabled streets to accommodate a substantial increase in traffic without seizing up. Even cyclists are getting a slightly better deal from the traffic engineers, thanks to the 'All Change to Bikes' campaign, encouraged by Sir George Young, MP and supported by junior Environment Minister, Lady Birk. There is now a bike route through Hyde Park and a growing number of concessions to allow cyclists to wriggle through diversions and road blocks. Pedestrians have Carnaby Street and South Molton Street to themselves, more room in Oxford Street and Leicester Square and the benefits of the South Bank and other walkways.

Some suggest banning cars from central London, perhaps forgetting that an estimated 230,000 are actually owned by people living in the centre. Euston Road, the Embankment and Park Lane are bad enough already without having to bear all the diverted traffic. More important is the argument that traffic is the life-blood of central London. Alan Cryer, who as chief city engineer of Westminster City Council is responsible for 5,334 acres of the centre, reckons that more restraint could be damaging.

> One of the main concerns of this council is with the economic base of the city and the possible decline of the rate base as firms move out. Movement is vital to economic activity: people have to get to work, shops need deliveries, businessmen travel about during the day. If people and goods can't move, firms will leave the centre.
>
> In the past five years all the major traffic schemes have been environmental improvements. Whatever you think of Oxford Street as an improvement for buses, taxis and pedestrians, it has made life extremely difficult for the rag trade of the surrounding streets because of the extra congestion. Proposals from the GLC like 'speedbus', involving almost total priority for buses to the detriment of other road users, fill this council with horror. It

could be extremely damaging to shops and businesses in the streets affected.

For the next ten years there will be very little capital to build roads, so the concentration should be on making the best use of the roads we have. I don't think that is achieved by effectively sealing off two lanes of a road for perhaps ten buses an hour in each direction.

One of Alan Cryer's personal enthusiasms is for the jitney – a cross between a bus and a taxi which would carry destination signs, but could be diverted by the passengers to suit their requirements. The suggestion has support from Bill D'Arcy, general secretary of the Licensed Taxi Drivers' Association, although other unions are not so keen. D'Arcy is certain that there will be a continuing demand for taxis, but a change in the way they operate: 'The GLC hasn't the resources to improve bus services, and people are going to demand more personal mobility at times when they don't necessarily want to use their cars – when they've had a drink, for example.'

Bill D'Arcy also favours allowing cab-sharing, a suggestion put to the Maxwell Stamp committee of Inquiry in 1968. But there will be problems:

It's nonsense when you see a queue of a hundred people at Victoria and you take one person to Oxford Circus, when you can bet your life there's another three or four going there. One problem about taxi-sharing that would have to be got over is the public's attitude: if you carry four people from Victoria Station to King's Cross Station, all strangers, they may have stood in that taxi queue for half an hour. You go from A to B and we'll say that there's 60p on the meter. If you say to each passenger, 'Right, it's 30p each' – that's half what's on the meter – I guarantee one, at least one, will say, 'Hold on, there's only 60p on there and you're going to get twice that amount.' They don't think that they've gone from A to B at half the normal price. They say, 'This is wrong if this guy gets more than he should'. But if it was all laid down, then they'd accept it.

City cash

Quite a number of those dashing about in taxis are City men, and it is impossible to discuss central London without considering the Square Mile. It has only 6,000 residents, but about 400,000 people work there. It elects its own Lord Mayor (who has considerably more prestige than the Chairman of the GLC), has its own police force, its council does not split on party political lines, and is vital economically, both to London and the country. In 1975/76, over seventy-five per cent of the £162 million of rates raised on the offices and other property in the City was distributed to services throughout Greater London. And without the millions earned by insurance, banking, ship brokerage, commodity trading and other City activities (£1,077 million in 1975), Britain's balance of payments would look even less healthy than it does.

All this concentration of capitalist power is extremely offensive to the Left of the Labour Party. Nationally, there are moves to take over the banks and insurance companies because the Left believes that too much of the nation's savings is channeled into property and other apparent fripperies and not enough into industry. This charge is denied by the City, which says if the Government did not borrow so much, interest rates would come down and firms could afford to take loans. Locally, the GLC's Labour administration voted in February 1977 to abolish the City's local government powers, and spread them around the poor surrounding Labour boroughs such as Tower Hamlets, Hackney, Islington and Southwark. There is little prospect of this happening, mainly because even a Labour Government is terrified of the international consternation which might be caused by the prospect of a major shake-up in the City. It is fair enough for Sir Harold Wilson and his committee to review the functioning of the financial institutions after the criticism about the unacceptable face of capitalism. But anything more drastic might start a run on the pound.

Perhaps the greatest defence of the City is that it works, at least in the way that a mixed economy works. The justification for the City Corporation is that it looks after the interests of City firms, fighting the GLC to allow new premises to be built, for example.

At the moment, foreign banks are queueing to establish branches in the City. The Baltic Exchange earned £146 million in 1975, Lloyds is the one place in the world where you can be sure of insuring an oil rig or a communications satellite, and the commodities market is trading furiously in everything from soya beans to copper. With all due respect to the councillors of Tower Hamlets, Hackney and Islington, who are seeking to take over the City Corporation's powers, I do not feel they have the interests of the Square Mile at heart.

The best policy for central London over the next few years is to let the City and West End get on with those operations they handle best: offices, shopping, tourism, entertainment. Planners should be cautious of resisting too strongly the pressures for change, and seeking to impose their own visions. The lessons of what can easily happen are there to see around the edge of the centre, amid the inner city.

THE INNER CITY

The inner city hit the headlines in 1976. In September a Cabinet Committee was formed to consider the problems of inadequate schools, racial conflict, unemployment, inadequate housing, poor environment – all factors which have contributed to the violent disruption and decline of American cities and are already evident in Britain. The Environment Secretary, Peter Shore, made speeches which were interpreted to mean that the Government was considering cutting back on New Towns projects so that funds could be channeled into inner areas. Newspaper and television journalists began to realise that a wide range of complicated and depressing stories could be packaged up as a new cause for concern.

Over the next six months the ills of Glasgow and Liverpool, Birmingham and Bradford were catalogued in great detail. The centre of Liverpool has been devastated by insensitive council redevelopment, families shifted to new estates on the edge of the city, while acres are left derelict. Unemployment among male Liverpudlians was thirty-three per cent in some areas, mainly because of the decline of the docks and the failure to attract new jobs to the centre. Council officials, community workers and politicians were reported to remark privately that there was little hope for the area. Glasgow was found to be even worse, with Clydeside leading the national deprivation league table. A £120 million Glasgow Eastern End Renewal Project is under way to bring in new housing and industry. Regional and local government have been pressed into an alliance to carry out the scheme. It is a formidable task. Joblessness has become a way of life for the men, truancy for the children. Alcoholism and vandalism are rife. Throughout the country the pattern seemed the same. People and industry have moved out, local councils have knocked down old homes and put up estates which house large numbers of unemployed, single parent families, immigrants.

The Labour GLC, which could never resist a passing bandwagon, produced its own brochure in which the Leader, Sir Reg Goodwin, warned: 'Events over the past year have shown that there is now a real danger of social unrest fuelled by justified resentment at the tragedy of high unemployment and inadequate services. The possibility that London might follow the cities of North America into a descending spiral of social and economic decline accompanied by civil disorder on a scale we have not previously encountered in this country is now real enough to justify urgent intervention'. He reproduced the now-familiar statistics of loss of industrial jobs (ten per cent unemployment in Stepney, Poplar and Deptford), homelessness, empty property and high rates, and made the usual call for the Government to stop trying to ship London's industry off to Liverpool and Glasgow. The overall effect was marred when Tory leader Horace Cutler discovered that several of the photographs of the 'unacceptable face of inner city life' were taken by Shelter in

Liverpool, not by the GLC in London. But that, of course, was an even better story.

Columnists played the usual game of rowing against the tide. Joe Rogaly wrote in the *Financial Times* under the headline, 'Let the centres of cities wither away': 'The decay and disintegration of our inner cities has not gone far enough. We should do everything we can to speed up this process; all talk of resuscitation should be replaced by a more down to earth consideration of what people really want.' He suggested that since people and firms clearly want to move to the suburbs and villages it was folly to pour more money into rebuilding the inner cores of cities.

Mr Rogaly is a good man with the ringing phrase and warned Peter Shore that money, where spent, should be concentrated on quite specific areas and individuals in need: 'It could be that the death-knell of twentieth-century civilisation is its refusal to acknowledge in time that the large concrete and asphalt tribal areas that we have created cannot be tolerated for long by normal human beings.'

For politicians and the media, the inner city has belatedly become the best urban sob story since *Cathy Come Home* helped launch the National Campaign for the Homeless. None of the problems are new. They have simply been intensified by the current recession with consequent higher unemployment and fewer public funds. The first Environment Secretary, Peter Walker, set up six studies in April 1972 to look at the issues in detail, but it was only last year that his successors at the Department of the Environment began to display any great interest in them. Was it only coincidence that the Cabinet Committee was announced a week after there were riots between West Indian youths and police at the Notting Hill carnival? Well, actually, yes. The Prime Minister, James Callaghan, had tried to interest journalists in the story of the Committee in July but had found few takers. Only when newspapers were searching for a follow-up to the riot did the Committee assume any importance in the media.

This note of cynicism is not intended to devalue the genuine concern of Ministers and journalists, but to show that once a major story is running there is a tendency for stereotypes to dominate the debate. All housing problems become those of Cathy, all road building is equated with destructive motorway construction, all inner city problems get identified with the wasteland of Merseyside. For London this is particularly dangerous, for while the capital's problems may show some similarities with other cities, there are considerable differences, and different policies may be appropriate.

Limited resources

Some pointers to future Government policy were given in February 1977 when Peter Shore spoke at a conference in Bristol entitled 'Save

Our Cities'. He suggested that industry should be preserved where it exists, and more established in areas such as London's Dockland; small firms should be encouraged, training provided for unskilled workers, environmental and social services improved, homes made available for purchase as well as for rent. On the practicalities of achieving these ends, Mr Shore suggested that local and central government partnerships might be established, or new agencies founded. Instead of the large numbers of small-scale initiatives of recent years – like the Community Development Projects, the Urban Programme, the Comprehensive Community Programmes – Mr Shore proposed a new corporate approach. The resources of the main housing, education, social service and transport programmes must be integrated, and more emphasis given to spending on the inner city, he said. The sting was in the tail: although it was desirable to ensure 'some additional and carefully directed resources for the inner city', he added: 'there is, I regret to say, no extra money available waiting to be earmarked for inner cities.' Despite a passing reference to Docklands, there was little in the speech for London. In fact, Mr Shore specifically warned that priority must go to the north. For local authorities who have been accustomed to trying to spend their way out of trouble, this was bad news. It struck a rather different note from the Tory Reform Group, which had urged spending £100 million a year within a decade.

In the national context, there is some validity in the Government decision to play down London's problems in comparison with those of Glasgow and Liverpool. The capital is still relatively buoyant, and while there are pockets of unemployment the situation is not as bad as elsewhere. Although a survey of sixty employment exchanges in London showed unemployment in twenty of them to be ten per cent above the national average, this percentage, and worse, existed in forty-four out of fifty-six exchanges in Glasgow.

Docklands: the empty acres

London is similar to Liverpool and Clydeside, however, in that all three cities have lost port trade and suffered a massive decline in docks and riverside industry. Docklands is a vacuum waiting to be filled, but other parts of London's inner city, such as Hackney and Wandsworth, Kilburn and Brixton, present a different picture: they remain overcrowded, with small scope for substantial factory developments, little play space for children and heavy pressure on housing.

Peter Shore's predecessor, Anthony Crosland, made the Government's position on Docklands clear in a White Paper in 1975. The GLC and the Dockland boroughs of Tower Hamlets, Newham, Southwark, Lewisham and Greenwich were given the same message as the Bristol conference: any money must come from reshuffling existing budgets. The councils were pressing for money because over the past ten years St Katharine Docks, London Docks and Surrey Docks have closed down, and trade has fallen throughout the area from Tower Bridge to Beckton. This has not only cost thousands of dockers their jobs, but has bereft the entire area of its vitality.

In 1971, Peter Walker and the then Tory Leader of the GLC, Desmond Plummer, announced jointly that independent consultants would prepare plans for the 5,000 acres of Docklands. When these were published two years later they met such opposition from local groups that the Labour administration which took over at County Hall that year scrapped them. Instead, it set up a new joint committee consisting of the GLC and the Dockland borough councils. The subsequent proposals for a new tube line, housing, industrial estates and parks have been the result of an extensive public consultation exercise, and depend upon the investment of considerable sums of public, as well as private, money.

There has already been some activity to the west of Docklands, particularly at St Katharine Docks where Taylor Woodrow have built a very attractive World Trade Centre, marina, hotel, flats and yacht club, making use, in part, of converted warehouses. But that scheme was under way before the Docklands planning exercise, and has succeeded because of its position close to the City. It has succeeded, it should be said, against the odds, because although the project was started under a deal negotiated with a Tory GLC in the 1960s, opposition from Labour in 1973 nearly sank it. Next door, in London Docks, there is a promising scheme under way for what amounts to a new village of Wapping. The Labour controlled borough council of Tower Hamlets, under its leader Paul Beasley, overcame its distrust of developers and has teamed up with Jeffrey Sterling's Town and City Properties and the Port of London Authority to build homes, offices, factories and parks. The ultimate success of both the St Katharine and London Docks schemes will depend upon the injection of large sums of private capital, particularly into offices and display areas which are near enough to the City to be profitable. These commercial elements help pay for the houses and amenities. Unfortunately, developers are far less attracted to areas of Dockland such as the Surrey Docks on the south bank and Newham to the east. Roads and public transport are poor and development costs are high. Both Southwark and the GLC were prepared to sign up with an American firm, Trammell Crow, for an enormous wholesale supermarket operation in Surrey Docks, but in 1976 the Americans shelved the scheme because of financing problems.

The GLC has pleaded with successive Environment Secretaries that little will happen in Docklands unless the new River Line tube is built east-west through the area from Fenchurch Street to Thamesmead, the GLC's own new town on the Erith marshes at the eastern end of Docklands. Public money is also needed to buy sites, build roads and housing, and generally clear up a century's industrial refuse. Although the story is not very different from Merseyside, and prompts similar prescriptions, the response of the Government has been that Liverpool has more problems than London, and the capital should be big and rich enough to find much of the necessary money itself. If a new Thames road-crossing is to be built at Thamesmead, then somewhere else must do without a by-pass. On this sort of analysis, the future of Docklands is fairly bleak. But if the worst happened, it would be possible to fence around the empty dock basins and forget them. No such option is open for the rest of London's inner areas where the problems – and, fortunately, the possible solutions – are different.

Stockwell: the crowded core

The Shankland Cox Partnership and the Institute of Community Studies were commissioned by Peter Walker in 1972 to study Stockwell in Lambeth as one of six inner area studies through the country. Their reports have been appearing, without much publicity from the Department of the Environment, for the past few years and have now been assembled in a book called *Inner London – Policies for Dispersal and Balance*. The authors, Graeme Shankland, Peter Willmott and David Jordan, turn many of the inner city arguments on their heads. Instead of calling for the wide-scale re-establishment of industry to provide jobs for the unemployed, they assert that many people living in inner areas would prefer to leave for the suburbs or the New Towns, where they would have better and cheaper homes and more chance of a job. With fewer people living in Stockwell it would be easier to cope with the violence and vandalism which sprang from too many bored children living on overcrowded estates. Pressure on housing would be reduced, so there should be no objection to middle-class families moving into the area to try and improve property.

The area, east of the new Covent Garden market at Nine Elms and south of the Oval, is typical of many developed in the last century. Two hundred years ago, Stockwell was a small village on the edge of London, with its own manor house, lesser gentry grouped around the green, and a few dozen workers' cottages. There were open fields up to the edge of the city at Kennington. The village grew, until it eventually merged with London. Some small 'oases' of imposing homes for well-off refugees from the City were established – a small circus at Lansdowne Gardens, a crescent at Stockwell Park and around a small park at Durand Gardens. Later, a mass of cheaper houses and flats were built. Some of the more imposing houses have

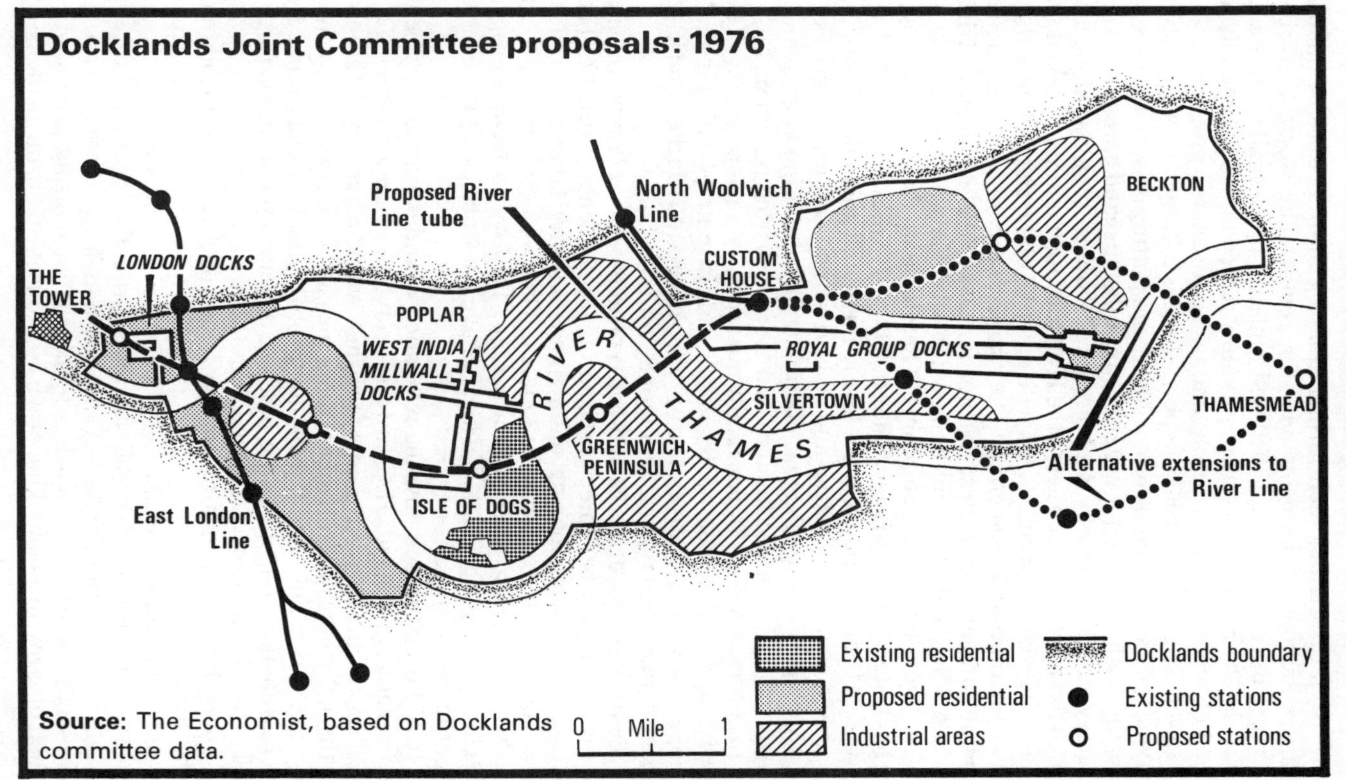

Source: The Economist, based on Docklands committee data.

now been restored to their former glory by those colonising middle classes looking for bargains near the centre. The worst Victorian terraces have been demolished and replaced by council estates and schools; the rest is a mixture of privately rented housing, generally in need of repair and conversion, and owner-occupied property.

In one street, the authors report, there is a couple in their sixties paying only a few pounds rent a week, and putting up with the lack of a bath, wash basin or hot water because the husband earns little as a factory labourer. Nearby is a Member of Parliament, living alone in a small flat because he can get to the House in eight minutes. Next door is an advertising executive, his wife and two children in a house they have restored and converted. They have two cars, two bathrooms and all kitchen appliances; but not far away live a Northern Irish couple who have fled from Belfast and struggle with their family in three damp, mouse-ridden rooms. They have no kitchen, bathroom or hot water, and no privacy. They had hoped to move out of London:

> We've been to Andover. It's lovely there – all green fields, fresh air and everything's clean and new. It's quite different from this place. This is a rough area, not a nice place to bring kids up in, with lots of problem families and stereos blaring out all night.

In contrast, a West Indian family not far away is happy to stay. The husband, a skilled motor-fitter, has installed central heating in their house. They have relatives nearby, shop in Brixton Market, and have spent a great deal of time and money on their home.

Shankland Cox describe another typical inner city family – a wife living alone with her three children on supplementary benefit. The accommodation is appalling: damp rooms, a shared lavatory, no bath. She said: 'It's so hard for the kiddies. They've nowhere to play. I wish I could get a place with a garden. I'd love to have a proper kitchen with a proper sink. I'd like to have hot water. I'd like to have electric plugs in the room.'

It is difficult to see how the relaxation of industrial development certificates, giving the GLC powers to advertise London as an industrial centre and to make grants for firms, would make any difference to these families' lives. If any of these measures succeeded in attracting large scale industry, they would probably make things worse by increasing the competition for housing. Shankland Cox argue forcefully that fewer people are needed in the area, not more.

There are particular problems with the large numbers of children who have nowhere to play. A survey shows that they are concentrated in the council tower blocks, and the older five-storey, walk-up estates which have become dumping grounds for single parent families. The streets are dirty, vandalism and mugging are increasing. Although Lambeth council has a substantial housing programme, much of it involves knocking down old houses and using up housing vacancies on those displaced. The council has a waiting list of 17,000 households but in the past three years housed only 572 of them, despite building 1,626 new homes and converting 502 others. Fewer people in the area would allow more hope of reducing the waiting list.

About a third of those interviewed said they wanted to move out of London. About a quarter said they were actually planning to leave. The main reason for not going was that they did not want to change jobs. Attachment to the area or to the people was far less important, and only one per cent mentioned the proximity of Stockwell to central London as a reason for staying.

Decentralisation policies have failed in the past, the authors say, because they have encouraged the most skilled to follow the most enterprising firms away from the inner city. Nationalised industries have cut staff; in consequence those left behind found fewer factory labouring jobs and less chance of working for the gas, electricity or water boards or British Rail. West Indian youths, who traditionally have favoured industrial employment rather than the office and other commercial jobs, have swollen the unemployment figures. Their families cannot escape the inner city because they cannot afford to buy a home elsewhere, there is little to rent privately, and it is almost impossible to transfer to council housing outside the area. Few families living in the suburbs would wish to swap a semi-detached council house for a tower block in Brixton. Travel to other parts of London where there may be jobs is not easy by public transport.

Shankland Cox carried out a survey of firms in the Stockwell area which convinced them that there was only limited scope for more industry. Although new firms were opening, more were leaving or closing, mainly because Stockwell is too built up to allow for expansion and those looking for jobs generally lacked the necessary skills; consequently firms leave their old, damp multi-storey factories which need new heating, lighting and ventilation and make for suburbs or New Towns. Or else they simply die. Shankland Cox sum up the situation:

> It may seem paradoxical that labour shortage was a problem at all for firms, given what we have reported earlier about unemployment. The key to the paradox lay in the mismatch, confirmed in the interviews with employers, between the skills that were available and those the firms actually needed. Some of these skills were scarce nationally, electrical engineers being an example; others, such as clothing machinists, were local. Some firms had labour problems because they paid low wages; others because their factories were inaccessible, insalubrious or in areas that were run-down or lacking facilities such as lunch-time eating places.

Complementary policies

Although Shankland Cox suggest that efforts should be made to retain industry and train unskilled workers, they argue that a more fruitful source of jobs will be small-scale operations: 'In Lambeth and inner London these enterprises take many different forms – small, full-time manufacturing, women working at home, street traders, independent professionals, family shops, mini-cab drivers, cobblers, tailors and plumbers.'

Their main conclusion is that there is the need for a balance between improvement of the inner city, and continuing support for the dispersal of population:

> The GLC has recently suggested that expenditure on New and Expanding Towns might be cut back to release public resources for urban renewal in Docklands and other parts of London. We would argue that dispersal and urban renewal are complementary policies and that London needs greater resources for both, but if resources cannot be increased then the main emphasis should be upon new housing outside inner London. The cost of rehousing an inner Londoner in inner London is much higher than rehousing him elsewhere and there is no shortage of prospective emigrants.

From this analysis, Shankland Cox draw conclusions not all of which mean spending more public money than is currently available. The main suggestion is that council homes should be built, or houses bought by councils in the outer boroughs so that families could move from Lambeth to areas such as Croydon, Sutton and Merton. If necessary, housing should be built in the Green Belt. Stronger links should be established with the New Towns, and arrangements made for families to move there. It may well be better to be living on supplementary benefit in Harlow than in Stockwell. Only in this way will it be possible to give those dissatisfied with life in Stockwell what they want, at relatively low cost. At the same time, the movement to inner London of middle class families prepared to buy and improve property should not be discouraged – surveys showed that most of the locals did not resent this, and in fact welcomed the uplift to the area provided by more private money.

In January 1977, at a press conference organised by Housing Minister Reg Freeson to present summaries of three inner city studies, Sir Reg Goodwin said he rejected the Shankland Cox conclusion because GLC studies did not support the assumption that there would be jobs for the unskilled in the suburbs and New Towns. A less charitable explanation of the GLC's unwillingness to embrace the Shankland Cox proposal is that little agreement has been reached with outer London boroughs on transferring inner London residents to them. The GLC's own scheme for helping workers move to New and Expanding Towns is widely criticised as inadequate, and is being run down. It is doubtful if the Tories would be sympathetic towards the proposal either, since they are opposed to further council housing in the suburbs.

Some of the Shankland Cox improvements, such as more play spaces, improved rubbish collection, a major expansion of training schemes and better social services would cost money. Furthermore, the poverty which afflicts more than one in five of the households in the area will only be tackled, the consultants suggest, by higher child benefits and pensions.

These proposals are not simple to carry out, but they are a lot easier than competing with other regions for major industrial employers whose very existence will be in doubt until the national economy considerably improves. Many of the Shankland Cox proposals could be adopted in areas like Stockwell, given the political and bureaucratic will at central and local government level. Dockland is, on the other hand, much more problematic. There, the choice is spend large sums of private and public money on establishing new jobs, homes, parks and schools, or abandon the area.

At present, the prospects for individual areas of Docklands are mixed. Tower Hamlets is getting on well with the developers Town and City, but there must be doubts about whether their promised offices – which would have been highly profitable five years ago – will be built for some years. Until they are, the private developer can hardly make a major contribution to the cost of housing and parks. Southwark has been left high and dry by the withdrawal, temporary or otherwise, of Trammell Crow from the Trade Mart project, leaving the centre of Surrey Docks blighted by uncertainty. Newham has reached agreement with the GLC on building some 8,000 homes at Beckton, half put up by the local authorities, the rest either by private builders or housing associations. There is commercial interest in establishing a major new shopping centre in the east of the area, and hopes that the new industrial estate being developed by County and Suburban Properties will be let. Few, if any, of the borough planners believe that the proposed River Line tube will be built, although both Labour and Conservative groups at County Hall remain entranced by the prospect and claim it is essential to regeneration of the area. The Tories have some vague notions of further schemes like the St Katherine's project, but no details have been worked out.

The grand vision has faded. Docklands is yet another case of 'if only': perhaps the acres of devastion would now be part-transformed if only there had been agreement in 1970 to go ahead with a number of existing small-scale plans. But the London disease has struck again: boroughs, GLC, Government, Tory, Labour could not agree, and the result has been stagnation.

THE SUBURBS

Meanwhile, the suburbs are more typical of tomorrow's London than either the centre, or the decaying inner areas. The trends for people to move out, drive to work, buy homes all create a suburban life style.

Depending on your point of view, that means a uniform mass of semi-detached, middle-class drabness or the dreamland a few stops down the line where homes have gardens. To some extent it is fair to generalise about the twenty outer London boroughs which form a ring around the inner city and are themselves encircled by the Green Belt. They have many similarities: more people own cars than in the rest of London, there is more open space, the houses are in better condition, the schools are controlled by the individual local council rather than by an overall authority as in inner London. There are, of course, differences. Working-class Barking has little in common with the Borough of Richmond. Some suburbs, like Harrow, grew up as residential dormitories when new tube or railway lines opened to carry commuters to City offices; others, such as Hillingdon which includes Heathrow Airport, have their own economic base.

But the lure of the suburbs is a common one. Take Bexley, for example. It encapsulates much of the likely structure of outer London in the 1980s and 1990s, with already three households in five owning a car, and one in ten, two cars. Over two thirds of families own their home. Clerks, managers and professional people commute to central London, but many work locally. There are also substantial numbers of electricians and engineers working in the area because of the industry in the north of the borough.

People can buy a three-bedroom house there for about £15,000 and commute into central London on a season ticket costing about £200 a year. Having settled down, they make considerable efforts to pull the ladder up after them and preserve the suburban comforts they have won. They resist the idea of a large GLC council estate being built down the road for fear it may become a ghetto of problem families exported from inner London. Nor do they welcome new, privately developed estates which would put more children into the school, add to the traffic, and increase the rates bill. The Tory council has calculated that the extra rates paid by the newcomers even when added to central Government grants would not counterbalance the additional costs. On those grounds alone it would happily refuse planning permission for all new residential development if it did not think that the Department of the Environment would grant permission on appeal anyway. So there is a limited amount of new building.

Bexley builds an average of 200 council homes a year and reserves them as far as possible for local people. Some twenty per cent of nominations for new homes and relets are given to the GLC each year as a gesture towards helping the problems of inner London, but these are not always taken up. Bexley suggests this is becuase the inner London families are being too fussy, while the GLC counters that they are being offered the borough's less desirable properties. The attitude of 'Bexley for the locals' is shared by both parties on the local council (this is just one of the ways in which Labour at County Hall does not always see eye to eye with Labour in the suburbs.) Nevertheless, Bexley – and other outer London boroughs – will soon have to face the fact that life cannot revolve exclusively around the inter-war family semi. As more and more young people take jobs in Marlowe House near Sidcup station and offices elsewhere, there will be an increasing demand for flats. And more elderly people will want to move to smaller houses once their children have grown up. Just as there is resistance to any major new building, so too there is redevelopment which, throughout the London suburbs, has taken the form of private developers buying up and demolishing large houses set in big gardens to build flats. An alternative for Bexley and other councils would be to encourage more conversion of houses into flats. Many houses will in any case need some work done to them as they become more than 60 or 70 years old by the end of the century, and with several people responsible for the repairs, the expense could be shared.

Both housing and employment in the suburbs will be affected by travel costs. If season tickets rise substantially, more Bexley residents will seek work nearer home, while some commuters from Kent may consider house hunting in Bexley to be nearer their work in central London. (In that situation, both homes for Kent commuters and jobs for Bexley residents will be in short supply.) In trying to provide extra office jobs the borough face the problem that the developers would like them to be at Sidcup, while the planners prefer them at Bexleyheath.

When the Greater London Development Plan was prepared, Bexley, like most other boroughs, was earmarked to have a strategic centre, and the proposals have now been approved by the Environment Secretary. The idea is that as London spreads it should develop new centres where offices, shops and entertainment can be concentrated near railway and bus stations. Some centres such as Lewisham and Wood Green have got under way quite successfully. Others, like Bexleyheath, are proving more troublesome. The station is half a mile from the proposed centre, which is inconvenient for office workers and shoppers, and the developers therefore tend to stick out for a site in Sidcup. As developers are fond of saying: 'There are three important components in a good office development, location, location and location'. However, Norwich Union is still interested in building a million square feet of shopping at Bexleyheath, with the prospect of major stores taking space. Work is due to start in 1979, if the compulsory purchase order is confirmed. The hoped-for-offices may also be built once the Department of the Environment grants an office development permit. Locals are hoping that once the centre is built, London Transport will improve the bus services. The more general problem about suburban centres is that they have been spread too thinly, on the basis that every borough must have one to satisfy local pride. However, potential new shopping is limited by the amount of money shoppers have to spend, and office developers are not keen to plunge into locations that may not thrive, and where firms may not be able to recruit staff. The result is that centres like Croydon and Sutton, which developers favour, may be told by the GLC that they have quite enough offices as it is, while Woolwich and Walthamstow are endorsed by the planners but cannot attract developers. It is only possible to nudge offices and shops into marginally attractive locations when demand is high and the development industry is buoyant. Bexley is determined that the jam must not be spread too thinly locally and the borough has periodic tussles with the GLC which wants to expand the shopping and office centre at its own new town of Thamesmead. Bexley feels that this might pull business away from the rest of the borough.

Another uncertainty for shopping centres is how increasing car ownership will change habits. As more and more people own cars, will they want to drive to discount superstores and load up with a week or two of shopping? Already a cash-and-carry store is prospering in nearby Bromley and there is likely to be pressure for more. The planners will be split between a concern to allow residents cheap and convenient shopping, and a fear that this will kill off other shopping centres. This reflects not just anxiety about the livelihoods of long-established shopkeepers – it could hit the council's finances. If bulk-buying really expands in suburban London the developers will probably look for larger, cheaper sites outside the London border. Nor does there seem much prospect that road building can match the increase in car ownership. The GLC is going to have such a tight transport budget that if it embarks on a large project such as the East London River Crossing at Thamesmead, there will be no money to cope with traffic congestion in Erith.

Extra dependence on the car will also pose problems for the young, the elderly, the disabled, and anyone else without a car. As more people drive to work or shop by car, bus services will become less profitable and less reliable. Cuts in services will have to be made as income from fares falls and the GLC and Government cut subsidies.

The residents may complain, but to a large extent they will have themselves to blame: public transport simply does not operate well when the predominant life-style is low density living and drive-everywhere travel. Residents do have some justification, however, in claiming that the boundary split between London Transport and London Country buses leads to lack of co-ordination of timetables and fares. Perhaps more adventurous entrepreneurs should apply to London Transport for licences to run private bus services at certain times of day. Without some prospect of alternative public transport, those without a car will have to stay at home, walk, or call an expensive taxi. The alternative would be a change of life-style for Bexley and the other suburbs and a major challenge for planners and councillors.

So even the attractive suburbs, the sugary outer edge of the doughnut, face potential problems which could eventually rebound on the centre and the inner city. What is certain, however, is that the three-ring city will remain a reality for the foreseeable future; and that since each ring fulfils a different function, their role and potential should be more clearly defined and recognised by planners, politicians, people who live in them – and people who want to migrate from one ring to another.

Suggested reading

Central London

Advisory Plan for Central London (Central London Planning Conference) The Plan consists of one technical and one policy document published in 1976 and available from the GLC bookshop.

The Heart of London, William Robson (Greater London Paper number 9, LSE 1965).

Inner City

Old Cities, falling populations and rising costs, David Eversley (GLC Intelligence Unit Quarterly Bulletin March 1972)

Inner Area Studies: Reports by Consultants and DoE. Summaries of consultants' final reports for Liverpool, Birmingham and Lambeth including Lambeth studies by Shankland Cox. (HMSO January 1977)

Cities in Crisis, David Lane (Tory Reform Group 1976)

Inner City, Nicholas Falk and Haris Martinos (Fabian Research series no. 320 1975)

Inner City, Graham Lomas (London Council of Social Services July 1974)

Inner London: Policies for Dispersal and Balance, report of an Inner Area Study in Lambeth, Shankland, Willmott and Jordan of Shankland Cox Partnership and Institute of Community Studies. (HMSO: forthcoming)

Strategy for Docklands by Docklands Joint Committee, 1976 (obtainable from GLC bookshop)

Suburbs

The Village in the City, Nic Taylor (Temple Smith 1973)

Suburbia, D. Thomas (Macgibbon and Kee 1972)
See also the topic papers on various subjects done in 1974/5 as background to Bexley's Borough Plan.
Household Interview Survey, a background paper for Enfield's Borough Plan (Enfield 1975).

LIVING IN LONDON

For most Londoners, the bright lights of the West End hold little attraction. Its theatres and restaurants, clubs and casinos are costly delights mainly for the seven and a half million foreign visitors who come each year to see the sights and scavenge the shops for bargains. It says much for the natural tolerance of the Londoner, beaten to a taxi or squeezed off the tube, that visitors still record that what they liked about the capital was the friendliness of the natives. This is not much comfort though for someone queueing irritably after work for an unreliable bus, with only a couple of cartons of Chinese take-away and *Kojak* on the box to look forward to.

Why suffer the inconvenience of the metropolis? Why not take a job in Bracknell, say, and swap the horrors of rush-hour travel for a leisurely drive to work, a cramped flat for a house with a garden? Why not indeed? Each year 350,000 Londoners decide to move out while only 250,000 provincials or immigrants think the streets are still paved with gold and move in to fill the gap. They find that the sense of fun which gave London a veneer of excitement ten years ago has gone: greyness has come with recession.

But for many families the disillusionment with London owes little to this loss of sparkle, or any hangover from an over-indulgent era. Those who want to leave usually have little to do with the bubbling centre and have always longed for a chance to move to the suburbs. Most of their troubles stem from the inability of planners and politicians to run the capital city machine efficiently, and to channel more of London's wealth into the streets and homes of areas like Wandsworth, Lambeth, Hackney and Islington. For many Londoners, housing, transport and schools seem more alluring further away from the still congested inner city. Planners and politicians bleat to Government Ministers that the raw material of their trade is deserting them at a staggering rate, and the flock could be down below six million in the 1990s; meanwhile, in the street, Londoners tell research

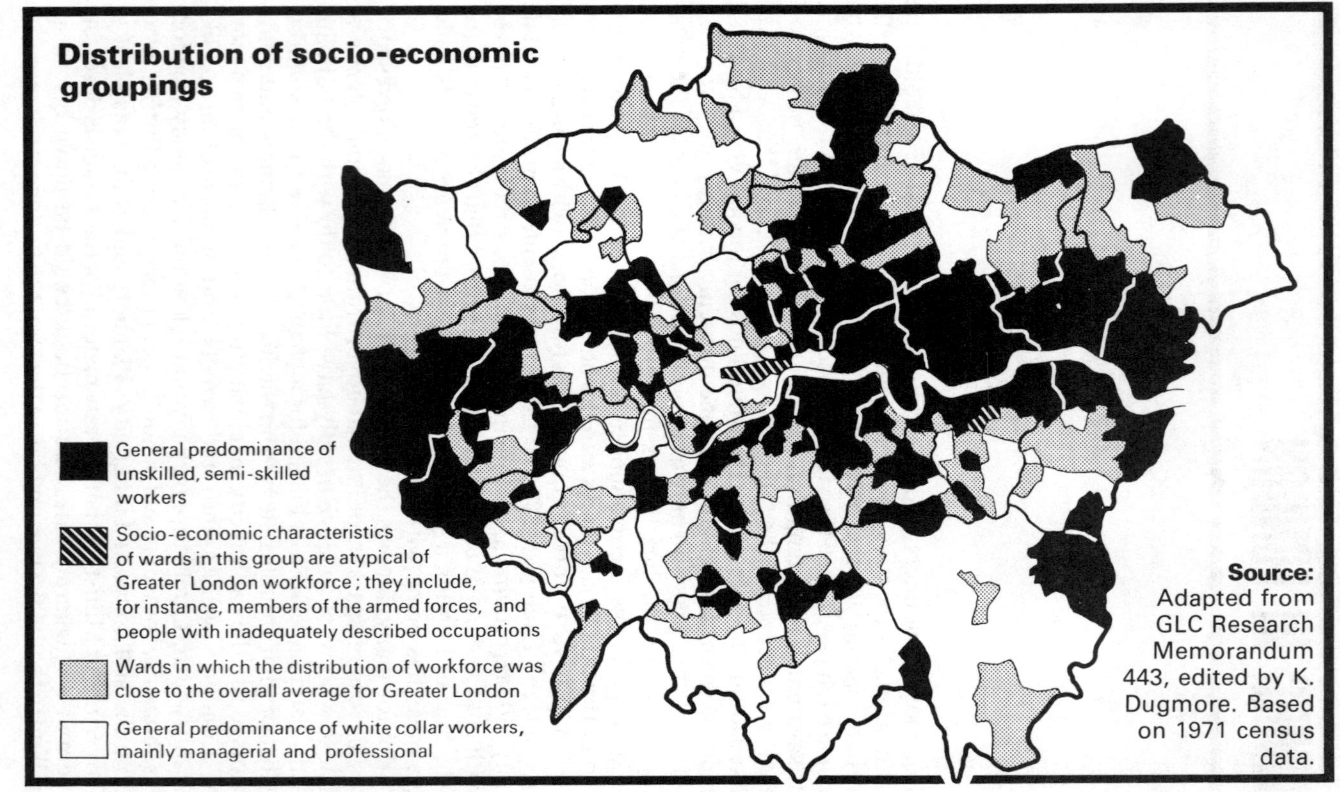
Distribution of socio-economic groupings
General predominance of unskilled, semi-skilled workers
Socio-economic characteristics of wards in this group are atypical of Greater London workforce ; they include, for instance, members of the armed forces, and people with inadequately described occupations
Wards in which the distribution of workforce was close to the overall average for Greater London
General predominance of white collar workers, mainly managerial and professional
Source:
Adapted from GLC Research Memorandum 443, edited by K. Dugmore. Based on 1971 census data.

teams that, but for their jobs, they would be off to the Home Counties and beyond.

Any councillor who can manage to digest an opinion survey can read the signs. Southwark council, for example, bravely asked its residents what they thought of the borough and what they would like. The result was a round raspberry for much that the municipality has in the past held dear. In an area where council building means that 70 per cent of property will soon be owned by Town Hall and County Hall, nearly 60 per cent of people questioned said they would like to own their own homes with their own patch of green, a few trees and somewhere safe for the kids to play. Some new council estates are most attractive, but Southwark residents have an over-riding impression of blocks of flats surrounded by boarded-up houses, and empty sites fenced with corrugated iron. The researchers commented:

> People told us about walls and lifts covered in graffiti, broken windows in empty houses and children smashing milk bottles. But it did not stop there because this kind of damage to property provoked fears – justified or not – about personal safety. As other work we have done has shown, this has become a key issue in city dwellers' attitudes to life, and it is of sufficient fundamental importance to make them wonder whether they should try to escape from an environment that has become threatening.

Urban violence

Police reports in 1976 confirmed fears that violence was on the increase, and it was quite often inflicted by the young on the old. John Wilson, Assistant Commissioner (crime), told a press conference: 'Iron bars, guns and pick-axes are often used against elderly people just for the sake of a few shillings left over after a drink at the pub.' Drug-taking had caught the headlines in the swinging London of the 1960s; by the mid-1970s, it was mugging.

Of course, things are not at all bad in Holland Park and St John's Wood, or further out in Barnet and Cheam. For anyone comfortably off, with an interest in the arts or simply tending the back garden, London can be a most pleasant city. The opera, theatre and galleries are unrivalled, restaurants not outrageously expensive. Certainly, central London is far safer and more salubrious than a hundred years ago, when an army of boys and girls, estimated at 100,000 wandered day and night 'destitute of proper guardianship, food, clothing or employment . . . in fair training for the treadmill and the oakum shed, and finally for Portland and the convict's mark'. These were the pickpockets and child prostitutes of the 1860s. In *London 1808-1870: The Infernal Wen* Francis Sheppard reports the French historian Hippolyte Taine's remarks after a walk down the Haymarket and Strand:

> Every hundred steps one jostles twenty harlots; some of them ask for a glass of gin; others say 'Sir, it is to pay my lodging'. This is not debauchery which flaunts itself but destitution – and such destitution! The deplorable procession in the shade of the monumental streets is sickening; it seems to me a march of the dead. That is a plague spot – the real plague spot of English society.

Today, the spectre raised by commentators is not of a return to the degradation of Victorian London, but of a capital city following this American prediction contained in *To Establish Justice, To Ensure Domestic Tranquillity (1969),* the final report of the National Commission on the Causes and Prevention of Violence:

> Central business districts in the heart of the city, surrounded by mixed areas of accelerating deterioration, will be partially protected by large numbers of people shopping or working in commercial buildings during daytime hours, plus a substantial police presence, and will be largely deserted except for police patrols during night-time hours.
>
> High-rise apartment buildings and residential compounds protected by private guards and security devices will be fortified cells for upper-middle and high-income populations living at prime locations in the city.
>
> Suburban neighbourhoods, geographically far removed from the central city, will be protected mainly by economic homogeneity . . . homes will be fortified by an array of devices from window grills to electronic surveillance equipment, armed citizen volunteers in cars will supplement inadequate police patrols in neighbourhoods closer to the central city. . .
>
> High-speed, patrolled expressways will be sanitized corridors connecting safe areas; and private automobiles, taxicabs, and commercial vehicles will be routinely equipped with unbreakable glass, light armour, and other security features . . . Armed guards will 'ride shotgun' on all forms of public transportation.
>
> Streets and residential neighbourhoods in the central city will be unsafe in differing degrees, and the ghetto slum neighbourhoods will be places of terror with widespread crime, perhaps entirely out of police control during night-time hours. Armed guards will protect all public facilities such as schools, libraries and playgrounds in these areas.
>
> Between the unsafe, deteriorating central city on the one hand and the network of safe, prosperous areas and sanitized corridors on the other, there will be, not unnaturally, intensifying

hatred and deepening division. Violence will increase further, and the defensive response of the affluent will become still more elaborate.

Ethnic groups

So far, there has been no justification for expecting quite this level of violence and discontent in London, although street crime and racial conflict has increased. Despite disputes between police and community workers on analysis of figures, there is no denying that unemployed West Indian youths are stealing a lot of handbags in Brixton, and did so at the Notting Hill carnival. But the violence is not one-sided: Pakistanis have been attacked in East London and Indians in Southall for no apparent reason. The seemingly deliberate decisions by councils to concentrate black families on older housing estates, also used as dumping grounds for all kinds of problem families, provide a potential battleground for race riots. What is amazing is that there has not been *more* trouble.

Tom Rees, until recently director of the Runnymede Trust, and now with the Home Office, maintains that there is considerable substance to charges that the police harass wide sections of the black community, not just the gangs of pickpockets.

> Black people are very philosophical about it in a way that most white people would find inconceivable. The only parallel that I can think of is about ten years ago when there was a big drugs scene among the young people. If you went to certain youth clubs, the chances of your being stood up against a wall and frisked were pretty high, whatever your colour. If you had long hair and were wearing jeans, the police instantly stereotyped you and you were in for it. Well, the blacks have got themselves into that position. The amount of damage to community relations that is done by say, a respectable black clergyman, well-known in his neighbourhood, being stopped and arrested in the street and taken off to the police station is enormous, and it is not uncommon. You can imagine what it would be like if your local vicar was continually being stopped and arrested by the police and taken to the police station, searched and disbelieved. That does happen to a lot of black people, who never dreamt of doing anything to bring them into conflict with the law.

Nevertheless it is true that one of the most startling and certainly the most highlighted aspects of the changing pattern of crime in London has been the crime rate among West Indian youths. The Metropolitan Police are concerned about the general increase in juvenile crimes amongst all groups, but insist that:

> Our records do suggest . . . that London's black citizens, among

> whom those of West Indian origin predominate, are disproportionately involved in many forms of crime.*

Nevertheless they believe that:

> In view of their heavy concentration in areas of urban stress, which are themselves high crime areas, and in view of the disproportionate numbers of young people in the West Indian population, this pattern is not surprising.*

Tom Rees sees the problems from a slightly different angle:

> Although the figures are very inaccurate and one can't be sure about them, there are signs that unemployment among young blacks in some parts of London is running at thirty or forty per cent, which is terrifyingly high. Visiting Americans say it is astonishing there have not been race riots in London, because in Detroit and Newark and other big American cities that kind of unemployment has triggered a very violent reaction.

The deprivation that many immigrants suffer in terms of bad housing, unemployment and poverty is made worse not only by their cultural differences and problems of adaption but also by the lack of positive action to encourage integration. Charles Boxer, Community Relations Officer in Wandsworth, is exasperated by people's attitude:

> Politicians have been conditioned to think of race as something you believe in, a moral issue. The Christians feel strongly about the brotherhood of man, socialists feel strongly about the brotherhood of all working peoples. We all say we have strong views about it, and say we're one race, the human race, and all that nonsense. We're on the believing track and we should be on the acting track.

Tom Rees believes that unless action is taken soon, the situation may become irretrievable:

> There has been a quite terrifying complacency about race. The minority groups have been quite small, relatively quiet, and concerned about earning their daily bread. Now the character of our cities is changing enormously. Something like thirty per cent of all births in some boroughs are to minorities, in many cases purely to coloured minorities, and these groups are going to become increasingly vociferous. Some local authorities – and the GLC is a good example – have woken up to the fact that problems lie ahead, but the majority still think there won't be any problems and that there is nothing very much they have to do.
>
> I'm not pessimistic in the sense that any of the problems which attend race relations either in Britain or in London are insoluble.

**Evidence of Metropolitan Police to Select Committee on Race Relations, 1976.*

But the time in which to solve them is running out and a lot of things have to be done. They have to be done in the employment field, in the housing field, in the education field and they almost certainly have to be done in relations between the blacks and the police. The longer the problems go unattended, the more likely it is that they will become intractable.

Each of the ethnic groups has its own problems. The hardships faced by West Indians are perhaps most apparent for they have a less stable family and social structure. Charles Boxer:

The main problem for the West Indians is that the family didn't really provide sufficient for the youngsters coming through. The value and importance of the family unit to immigrants, especially when they first arrive in this country, becomes more noticeable when one sees the lack of support that the West Indians have derived from their family structure, which tends to be weaker than that of many other immigrant groups. The breakdowns that result are, I suppose, fairly obvious. The parents came across here under great difficulties, fought their way up in a fairly hostile society, got the house, got jobs, not very good jobs – but they made it. They kept their heads down and went through a lot of strain and stress. It was a hard struggle. Their children didn't come across with them in the first place; they were left at home and tended to be brought across when the parents had settled down. By the time they came, the children were ten or eleven years old – what we call the one and a half generations, not first or second generation. Their parents had high expectations for them, thought they'd all be English people in the end, pushed them into school, thinking that the machinery would do its work and their children would come out the other end and be nice little employees. It did not work. The children came too late; the educational system was not geared to meet them and did not understand how to deal with them.

However, even now that most London children of West Indian origin are born in Britain, alienation between many parents and children persists. Tom Rees concurs:

There seems to be a particular problem with West Indian children through reasons which nobody is entirely clear about. It is almost certainly a combination of the cultural traditions which are fed into the family and the very intensive engagement in the economy by both parents. A very high proportion of West Indian mothers go out to work. There appears to be less parental support for West Indians than there is in most immigrant groups. The parents have encouraged their children to work hard at school, but maybe the kind of encouragement they have given has not always been well directed. They haven't been able to give the kind of help with homework and subjects that some white parents can give. I think that some parents have expected achievements that the school simply could not hope to offer the children. In addition, West Indian parents often have very strict standards of morality and a very puritan sort of work ethic; their children are reacting against all that and the school is encouraging a rather more relaxed attitude towards life. Conflicts between parents and children, which are normal anyway in the adolescent age, are much more intense among West Indians. On top of all that, I think the children have to some extent reacted against the jobs that their parents have done. They had been doing jobs which were not necessarily very unskilled, but are not very highly valued by society – London Transport workers, postmen, service industry workers, a lot of people working in hotels. The children have seen the jobs as society sees them, not tremendously full of status. They do not want to get stuck into that kind of job, and that has added to the tension with parents.

For almost all minorities, the difficulties of adapting are compounded by prejudice and discrimination. Tom Rees believes:

There's a hope which rears its head every three or four years in the press and elsewhere that discrimination is what happened yesterday, that today the world is an equal place and if you're black nobody is going to treat you differently because you're black. And every three or four years, there is a major research project to find out whether this is the case or not, and it still emerges that if you are black you have to try twice as hard to get even an unskilled manual job.

As pointed out in an *Evening Standard* article in February 1976, no one is providing the necessary initiative.

The complacency among employers and trade unions is enormous. Typically, both the CBI and the TUC have declared their opposition to discrimination but done nothing to ensure that their members work effectively to eradicate it. The TUC is even opposed to the one measure that would expose the extent of job discrimination: that is, requiring firms to keep open records of the number of black people they employ and in what capacity.

In housing, too, the minorities get a bad deal. A recent GLC survey of its own council housing in London acknowledged that 'non-white tenants are occupying a disproportionate share of older and less desirable properties'. A similar survey carried out by the Runnymede Trust yielded the same results. The accompanying report concluded:

The reasons for the present situation are of course complex, as this study recognises, and may well include an element of preference on the part of immigrant families. But though statistics do not accuse, neither do they excuse; surely it is time that all housing authorities looked critically at their own role in the process. This means all aspects of the allocation system, not least the attitudes of key officials such as housing visitors.

Latterly, the problems of getting a job have been intensified for groups who have relied on getting industrial rather than white collar work. As Tom Rees said:

> Industries have been moving out very fast, particularly from areas like the old East End and the industrial belt which goes up the Lea Valley, but also from south of the river both where the docks were and even as far as Wandsworth, Brixton and Clapham. These jobs have been mainly in the semi-skilled and unskilled sectors. They are jobs which are particularly useful to immigrants who come in without any large reservoir of manufacturing skills. To some extent, if you come from an immigrant group, even if you yourself aren't an immigrant but your parents were, your knowledge about and your ability to master a rather complex industrial system and the opportunities it offers will tend to be somewhat less than that of the indigenous population.

Faced with such a bleak future it is hardly surprising that many young West Indians tend to react violently. As already pointed out, the relationship between West Indians and the police is particularly strained; in some respects it epitomises the problems of adaptation on both sides of the community – ethnic minorities and indigenous population. Tom Rees:

> At the moment there is a very sour relationship, particularly between West Indians and the police, for which the police are not by any means entirely to blame, but for which they do carry a considerable amount of responsibility. In the Metropolitan Police, as in other police forces, there has been a division between the responsibility for what is known as community relations work and for ordinary policing, so that you have nice chaps, who are good at talking to black people and the press, doing community relations work. Then you have coppers who go around fingering collars. There isn't much prestige within the police force in talking to the press and talking to black people, whereas there is a lot to making arrests and being a hard man with a good reputation in the crime-busting front. What the community relations people say tends not to be taken too seriously by the crime people.

Indeed Tom Rees is worried that if the lot of the West Indians is not generally improved, a point of breakdown may be reached:

> There is a great deal of concern in London, quite rightly, about the development of black ghettos. I think it's right, because it's a bad thing not that there should be lots of black people living together, but that there should be a lot of black people living together in the conditions of failure, where there is a lot of crime, where the unemployment is very high, where the housing is lousy, where the future looks bleak.

Charles Boxer is no less concerned and points to what is already happening:

> A fair proportion of black kids are lost completely in society and nobody talks to them, they are completely alienated. One of the main problems with black youngsters is that they've got to have a social refuge amongst themselves, which keeps them away from the white community. They don't really impinge on the white community very much at all. They don't go round together. So you have a black late-teenage sub-culture building up which isn't really talking to whites and is losing its facility of doing so. At the same time the white population is not acquiring the ability to understand or talk to them. So put them both together – it's murder.

The hardships facing West Indians are perhaps more acute and in some ways different from those facing other ethnic groups. But one difference which does emerge is related only to time-scale. Charles Boxer:

> I think one of the worrying things about the Asian community at the moment is that they are tending to follow in the footsteps of the West Indian community and are starting to have some of the problems that the West Indians already face. The Asians seemed ideal immigrants. They built their bridgehead, they built their family structure, religious societies and their mosques. I thought that would last them some time and get them through the problems. The great thing about the bridgehead is that it becomes a centre of knowledge and enables you to manipulate life outside. But the bridgehead is breaking down and so are the Asian families and the kids. The children are no longer content with their parents' values. Another very important factor is that the Asian wives went out to work, giving them for the first time some independence, and this upsets the balance in the home. I think all the same things will happen to Asian kids: unemployment will be bad, the break-up of the home, leading to crime, alienation, drifting, youth culture.
>
> In addition, as many Asians, particularly those from East Africa, did not come to Britain by choice but were expelled from

their former homes for political reasons, there are many more elderly amongst them and for them the hardship of adapting is greatest.

An important factor in the breakdown of the minority communities is education. Charles Boxer referred to schools as 'the alien wedge in the Asians' bridgehead'. While on the one hand education should help children cope with social pressures, on the other hand, for many of the ethnic groups it is increasing the pressures by widening the gap between children and parents. The significance of these factors is greatest for London's schools because of the large numbers of coloured children attending them. Bev Woodroffe, the ILEA inspector for community relations, sets out the context:

> In the next ten years, the gradual decrease in the number of children entering school in Inner London will become a massive decrease, and that is the basis on which our thinking for the future has got to be done. The Registrar General's figures of live births to mothers from the New Commonwealth and Pakistan in 1973 indicated that between 22 and 25 per cent of children coming into the schools in 1978 will be from those groups. And those figures do not include other minorities' children whose parents were born over here. So I suspect that more than a quarter of children entering schools in 1978 will be from ethnic minorities. The evidence is that the children from these groups are not performing, by any of the normal sorts of tests and examinations, nearly as well as the indigenous population, even in the areas where they have settled or have been settled. The thinking used to be that if you could teach the children fairly quickly to function in English, they could get on in the classroom like anyone else.

The language problem persists, for, even though many children from minority groups are now born in England, they do not speak English at home, and language teaching does not solve the problems. Bev Woodroffe:

> We went through a period in the 1960s when our assumptions were that there was something wrong with the kids, and we had to do something with *them* so that they could make better use of our system. The shift now is to realise there may be something wrong with the *schools* that is stopping them getting the sort of education that they need. To give an example: if you grow up as an Asian child in an Asian family, living within a certain culture, a certain life style, used to certain ways of living; if you go into a school and find in that school nothing visually that represents you, that all the pictures are of white people, the teachers are white, the language they use is different, the expectations of behaviour are different . . . The curriculum in its widest sense

tends to debar certain groups from a sense of belonging to, involvement with and motivation towards the education that goes on in schools. I believe that one of the things it has done is to make us consider whether in fact the curriculum we have in our schools isn't too insular, even for the white children: I'm quite sure that it is – look at history or religion as taught in many schools. It is very selective in what it deals with, very selective towards its attitude to the past. There is a need for us to reassess what it is that we are teaching and how we are teaching, how we are relating past history to the present. More relevant, perhaps, would be for children to learn about current issues and their own environment.

PROPORTIONS OF MINORITY GROUPS IN THE CAPITAL

European	**Germany**	**Italy**	**Poland**	**Spain**	**Malta**
(a) UK total	157,680	108,980	110,925	49,470	33,840
(b) London total	34,300	32,545	32,505	25,640	8,305
(b) as % of (a)	22%	30%	29%	52%	25%
African	**Ghana**	**Kenya**	**Nigeria**	**Tanzania**	**Uganda**
(a) UK total	11,215	59,500	28,565	14,375	12,590
(b) London total	6,840	24,535	18,540	5,905	5,560
(b) as % of (a)	61%	41%	65%	41%	44%
American	**West Indies**				
(a) UK total	302,970				
(b) London total	168,695				
(b) as % of (a)	56%				
Asian	**Ceylon**	**Cyprus**	**Hong Kong**	**China + Formosa**	
(a) UK total	17,040	73,295	29,520	13,495	
(b) London total	8,470	53,095	6,865	3,815	
(b) as % of (a)	50%	72%	23%	28%	
	India	**Malaysia**	**Pakistan**	**Singapore**	
	321,995	25,685	139,935	27,335	
	106,380	8,520	30,135	4,460	
	33%	33%	22%	16%	

The numbers given are of people born in the countries listed but living in the UK.

Note: 13 per cent of UK residents live in London, but the proportion of minority groups in the capital is considerably higher:

Source: 1971 Census data.

Some recent projects are trying to bridge these gaps but their potential is limited by lack of resources:

> The ILEA support a number of Black Supplementary Schools. These are schools run by black people on a voluntary basis to give lessons and educational experiences of one sort or another, after school, at weekends, and in holidays. The teachers there tend to concentrate on English, maths and, very often, cultural studies. My experience is that they are well organised and well run by highly-motivated people who are learning to do something for themselves. We have got to learn from that, and see what elements in that situation can help the schools to develop the right approach. But one of the crucial things is that there are very few black teachers, very few black headmistresses or headmasters. There is not one black or Asian inspector among the hundred or so at the ILEA.

Highlife and low life

It is all too easy, though, to look at the problems of ethnic groups as if they were the dominant social factor in London life. There are many such coherent minorities – not all of them dissatisfied. London has attractions for others besides the tourist and the affluent. Despite redevelopment, there is still a sense of community cherished by older residents. The *Evening News* reported:

> Mrs. Florence Tucker, 53, from Rotherhithe, called London the greatest place on earth. 'I certainly wouldn't move out and neither would my neighbours. It's the friendliest place in the world. You've only got to stand in a bus queue or on the station and people want to chat.' Mrs Tucker has lived in Rotherhithe for 16 years. Before that she lived in the Old Kent Road. 'I leave my keys with a neighbour when I go out, knowing that I can trust her completely. There's certainly no shortage of things to do. We have bingo, the local and the civic hall. If you want any help you've only got to knock on someone's door. My daughter of 20 who lives with me wouldn't leave here for anything.'

Perhaps Mrs Tucker has hit the reason why those other 48 per cent do not leave London. They cannot resist bus queues. Life without the camaraderie of discomfort would not be the same. What is more typical than the stoical acceptance of delay reported by Georgina Walsh in the *Evening Standard:*

> At World's End the No. 11 broke down. At 8.05 am the gears juddered, and without a word spoken, the full load of passengers got to their feet, trooped off the bus and formed themselves into a queue at the Chelsea stop. Conductor Jerry O'Grady was in a daze. 'I didn't even have to ask them to get off. They realised

something was wrong, stood up and went of their own accord. Not a shred of trouble. Not a single complaint.'

Such is the stoicism and the discipline of the bus traveller. On the continent there would have been a riot, but as one passenger remarked drily: 'Who needs National Service when you've got London Transport.' It was 55 minutes before a relief vehicle arrived. The queue got bigger and piled itself all over the pavement; the faces got more set; the scrambles a little more frantic as time ticked by, and bus after bus arrived jam-packed, or drove straight on. Jerry O'Grady said sympathetically: 'I've counted nine or ten buses going by in 20 minutes. I tell you, if six came along in a bunch it would not be enough. You'd need 20 buses to clear that lot.'

On that bus it is a fair bet there was a secretary, a student, a waitress, – typical central Londoners tied to the capital by their jobs. But despite their common courtesy at the No. 11 bus stop, each has very different lifestyles.

For the secretary, working in a field where there are six job vacancies for every applicant, life in central London may be very congenial. It is a great marriage market, and accommodation is not too expensive if you do not insist on your own room. Jane Pooley described in the *Daily Telegraph* early in 1977 how she left Shropshire after four years as a reporter on a provincial evening paper, took a temporary job, and happily shared a room in Kensington.

> I knew no-one, and quitting my job, leaving home, and seeking success in London was the last resort on my list of options when attempts to get work in America failed. Naturally, I was apprehensive about the move: headlines about lonely bedsitter suicides, street muggings, high prices, commuter chaos, drug addiction revolved constantly in my mind.
>
> My fears were groundless. I love London life. I have found that the problems can be solved and the pitfalls side-stepped. Londoners are a fascinating cosmopolitan mix, too diverse to lump in any one category and London is a honeypot of delights – historical, cultural and in the entertainment field.
>
> Sharing is not only a financial necessity; it provides a ready supply of friends, confidantes and conspirators in misadventure. For the first time in my 23 years, I am fending for myself and it has been a shock to the system, and more specifically, the digestion. Food prices are high and I am tending to swing from wine, steak and asparagus tips at the pay-day end of the week to pizza and bread and jam for the rest.
>
> Career-wise, I am having to do temp secretarial work while I

look around. But I have made some good contacts and am convinced of the wisdom of the cliché that it is not what you know, but who, that counts. Any girl who can bash out a reasonably neat letter on a typewriter can make a living in London. On one memorable day, working as a temp secretary, my total output in eight hours was the making of lots of tea and coffee. My experience is not untypical.

Socially, London has been a relevation. My major problem at the moment is fitting in all the things I want to do and getting enough sleep to carry me through the next day.

Life may be fun for secretaries, but it is not so jolly for students worried about the value of grants, cuts in research projects and a lack of possible jobs at the end of the.course. When Mary Kenny visited the London School of Economics and University College, she reported in the *Evening Standard:*

> I came away with the impression of a serious-minded, hard-working, rather apprehensive generation of young people, who are confused, frustrated yet impotent. 'Everyone is very worried', said a 22-year-old history post-graduate at the Institute of Education, which trains teachers. 'Everyone is very frustrated because of these cutbacks and the general lack of jobs. My main worry is money and how I'm going to manage when I finish this year, and what will happen if I don't get a job. But I don't see what we can *do*: it's a question of economic reality.'
>
> His name is Daniel and he comes from Hackney, where his father is a security guard. (Like all the other students I spoke to, with the exception of those with official status on the NUS, he declined to give his surname, which I took as a further indication of how uptight and nervous students are nowadays.)
>
> Daniel wants to be a history teacher, but he would take a job in the Bank of England, where he has worked in holiday time, if he couldn't get a teaching post. In fact, he would be grateful for a management training job at British Home Stores where he presently works at weekends to supplement his £9 a week grant. His anxious and unsmiling views seemed very representative of the London student today.
>
> Gone are the angry revolutionaries, the energetic student activists of the late 1960s who appeared to threaten the whole order of bourgeois society in campus riots all over Britain. They nearly all appear to feel strongly about the squeeze on education, especially people who were aiming for an academic career. But there is an even deeper shock, possibly, at the root of it all. It took a 24-year-old Américan, at the School of African and Oriental Studies to see it clearly. 'British students have taken it

completely for granted that the Government will pay for their education – it was a natural *right* that the State should pay. Now, they are not so sure, and it comes as a fundamental shock to them.'

The students' problems are compounded by difficulties in finding somewhere to live; on grants they cannot compete for bedsitters with secretaries earning over £3,000 a year. The Rent Act of 1974 has made landlords reluctant to let to anyone who might appeal for a rent reduction as soon as they are in residence or use every wrinkle of the law to avoid eviction if they stop paying. Mary Kenny reckoned that the only way to get a flat in London of any sort was to know someone who would pass on a lease or allow you to stay while they were away, because they believed you would leave voluntarily. Landlords keep good property empty rather than let, and home hunters who are poor or do not know anyone pick up accommodation on another grapevine – the squatters' network. As newspapers began to realise that getting a flat is genuinely difficult, their attitude to squatters changed. No longer were they long-haired layabouts living on social security, taking drugs and challenging the fundamental rights of a property-owning democracy. Councils grant licences to groups of young people so they may live in and improve property awaiting redevelopment or renovation. The *Daily Telegraph,* which is usually fairly definite about its stereotypes of the young went so far as to headline an article by Stephen Platt: 'Well Done the Squatters', with only a small disclaimer that this was a personal view. Mr Platt reported that a survey in Haringey had shown that many squatters were British, employed, had tried to find accommodation and failed, and hoped to move out as soon as they could. 'Too easy to dismiss them as a damn nuisance' said the headline over Liz Forgan's assessment in the *Evening Standard,* which concluded that squatting was the one mobile and accessible area in the housing market:

> We have squeezed the housing market so tight that only people who conform to certain key shapes fit into it any more.

To buy a home, one needs to earn over £4,000 and have some capital, and councils are desperately trying to cope with waiting lists, tenant transfers and the claims of people displaced by redevelopment. For this reason, local authorities often have no room for those workers who serve the needs of the students, secretaries and tourists in central London. Behind the bright lights of the West End are some particularly tawdry problems. Angela Pitts described in the *Evening Standard* what lies above the cheery restaurants of Soho's Chinatown:

> The case of the Wong family in Lisle Street is typical. Mr and Mrs Wong and four of their children sleep in one bedroom,

roughly divided into two, while the other two sleep on a divan in the living area. But far worse than the overcrowding is the actual state of the building. In both rooms the ceilings are kept up by makeshift polythene supports. Water seeps through the rotting woodwork so that a bucket is permanently placed on the concrete living room floor. And the bathroom, shared by at least five other tenants, is permanently flooded. The rickety staircase leading to the first floor flat is unlit. The light bulbs were removed, says Mrs Wong, by the landlord and anyway the leaking pipes directly above the exposed wiring constitute a fire hazard to the whole house.

Mrs Wong says the children, particularly her three year old twin boys, are constantly being treated for throat and chest infections as a result of the permanent dampness and unhygienic conditions. Because of the pressure on the local GP, they have been seeing a specialist since the beginning of the year. They have been on Westminster council's housing list since November last year, but their application cannot be considered for a year after registration. Rent for the two room flat, plus kitchenette is £14 a week. As far as the council is concerned, the Wongs are one of the many urgent cases on its 8,000 housing list. But a spokesman confirmed that no inspection of the premises was made at the time of their registration:

'We have so many applications that it would be impossible to carry out inspections in every case. However, the urgency is assessed through correspondence between one of the council's medical advisers and the family doctor. In the case of the Wongs it was felt that their plight was less urgent than many other families on the list, so they were awarded relatively few points.' There is a statutory twelve-month gap for everyone registering on the housing list before their application can be considered.

Others working in the catering industry fare just as badly. The Low Pay Unit, an independent research body, reported that many of the men and women employed in West End hotels sleep rough and work in appalling conditions. Gareth Parry reported in the *Guardian:*

Of all the major industrial groups, the hotel and catering industry has the highest concentration of workers who are earning poverty wages. Because of the seasonal nature of the industry and also, it is expected, because of low pay, the industry has always relied heavily on casual labour. Catering workers are covered by legal minimum rates of pay, but there is evidence that many casual workers do not even receive the meagre rates to which they are entitled.

One washer-up in a pub was paid 40p an hour, and some of

the men had to pay as much as 50p to 60p a day in fares to reach their work. A casual worker is lucky if he gets a job on more than two days out of five and then only a minority are offered eight or more hours work.

The GLC estimates that the problem of low pay is widespread. Their research indicates that a quarter of London's 2,500,000 households are below a poverty line defined as £49 a week for a three-person family. 'There is genteel poverty behind the lace curtains', said Labour's deputy leader, Illtyd Harrington, with a sure eye for the headlines. The GLC maintains it has done something to help those in greatest need, like pensioners given free bus passes. The aim is admirable, and midday buses are crowded with the elderly. Some of the effects have been unexpected, however. The *Evening Standard* reported:

> Shrinking luncheon club queues were puzzling council officials in Sutton until they discovered that thrifty pensioners are joining a lunchtime gravy train across London for cheaper and bigger meals. Free bus passes are taking them five miles away to Tooting in the borough of Wandsworth, where luncheon club meals are a mere quarter of Sutton's prices. There, at 6½p a time, they can eat for a week for only a few pence more than their own borough's daily charge of 25p.
>
> But the bargain hunters are not going down well with Wandsworth's diners. They resent the 'first-come, first-served' procedure which means Wandsworth pensioners at the back of the queue get reserve canned food while early birds from Sutton get the meals of the day. Pensioners' meals organiser for Sutton, Mrs Connie Cracknell said: 'So that's where they are all going. At 6½p a time I can understand why they are doing it. Old people obviously shop around.'

Commuting

The pensioners are fortunate in having their fares paid. Other Londoners – and those who work in London but have moved outside to cheaper homes and a better environment – have been hit hard by a series of fare rises over the past two years. Long-distance travellers complain furiously that they have fallen into the great commuter trap laid by British Rail and Government. They were tempted out of town by what is, in terms of other capital cities, a highly efficient rail network. Once out on the end of the line their fares were put up by leaps and bounds. In October 1976, it was possible to commute 240 miles a day by using the 124 mph high-speed train from Bristol to Paddington, allowing a 7.30 am start from home and a 9.45 am start in the office. But by January 1977, the story was less cheery. Leslie Watkins reported in the *Daily Mail:*

John Oliver, personnel officer at the head office of a large clearing bank, last night endorsed a warning given by ASLEF boss Ray Buckton: 'Commuters, particularly long-distance commuters, are now being hit so hard that many are being forced to resign from secure jobs, because they simply cannot meet the travelling expenses.'

'There was a very vigorous campaign – by the railways and local authorities – to get us to live away from main centres like London', says 40-year-old Charles Hibberd, chairman of the East Kent Rail Passengers' Association. 'Countless thousands of people were deliberately lured into becoming commuters and now they find themselves in a sort of nightmare trap.' In 1963 his monthly ticket between Birchington and London cost £12. Now it is more than £50.

Even cutting travel costs by living in London does not solve the problem if your job is poorly paid. In September 1976 the *Evening News* reported:

Mr Charles Scott, ILEA's divisional careers officer for central London, said: 'The tragedy is that there are a lot of vacancies and more than enough unemployed youngsters to fill them. But it is impossible from a salaries versus fares point of view to bring the two together. Many are now asking for jobs near main line stations to avoid the extra cost of taking a Tube ride to their destination. But, of course, not all jobs are right on Liverpool Street's doorstep.'

Mr Scott gave an example of a 16-year-old boy from Epsom, Surrey who was offered a job as an apprentic engraver with a firm in Hatton Garden. His starting wage would have been £11.54 and his fares to work would have been between £8 and £9 a week. Naturally, the boy turned down the job. Another 16-year-old from Bexley, Kent rejected a job in a photographic laboratory offering a wage of £20 a week, because his fares would have cost almost one-third of his weekly income. A third school leaver in Hornchurch, Essex who wanted to train as a legal executive, made it clear that any job in central London offering less than £30 a week was not acceptable to him.

Working in London

As fares go up, employers find it more and more difficult to keep skilled workers. So there is increasing pressure on them to move their firms out of London where labour is more plentiful and there are better roads and lower rents. Remaining in London may be hard enough; trying to expand is even worse. Tommy Macpherson, managing director of William Mallinson and Downey Matt Ltd. in Hackney, says:

London has the most difficult, bureaucratic, slow and comprehensive set of building restrictions that I have come across anywhere in the world. We had one tiny job to do on one of our premises near London Docks, which should have cost only £900. Yet it took nearly three years for all the authorities to agree, from the fire authority down to the borough surveyor and back again, because if anyone changes anything you have to go back over the process with all of them. At the end of the day, what should have cost £900 cost about £4,000. Industrial warehouses are required to be built like Mecca ballrooms, and while that may be splendid for the environment and up to a point necessary for safety, it helps make London less competitive in Britain, and Britain less competitive in Europe. We estimate that building a £250,000 warehouse may be £80,000 cheaper outside London than inside, partly because the number of controls leads to over-design. Bureaucracies tend to be competitive – the borough competes with the GLC, the Fire Authority competes with the transport committee, and it is difficult to see either of them backing down. Altering the design when the job is in train is very expensive. The whole atmosphere has been one of prevention of activity. Only in the last six months have they panicked and tried to set up some machinery for promoting industrial activity because they can see London going the way of New York.

Many firms want to keep headquarters in London, but they need determination to reap the benefits of a capital city location. Peter Casemore, building projects manager at the Deptford branch of Molins, a firm which produces machinery to make and pack cigarettes, tells a similar story. Molins decided to stay and expand in Deptford, partly because of the advantages of having a head office in the capital. Peter Casemore says:

Our customers want to be able to see our operation as well as meet senior staff. If the President of a major tobacco company visits London, he may bring his wife and children. We can send a car to pick him up from his hotel and, while his wife and children do some shopping and sight-seeing, he can meet our top people and perhaps go on to tie up something with bankers in the City. It would take a lot of pressure to make us leave. But it has taken a tremendous amount of time to get our plans agreed, however sympathetic the authorities have been in principle. Over the past two or three years, when we have not been exactly sure what we wanted to do on the site, but knew certain things, we have invited to our premises virtually everyone from the Leader of the GLC downwards. A lot of time has been spent over the last few years by senior members in Molins showing people round and explaining what we want to do. This has paid dividends, and we have got the backing more easily. But it has taken a lot of time.

The one place which is most strongly resisting the pressure to decentralise headquarters operations is the City. One might think that telephones and computer links, visual display units and personal television circuits would allow the City man to give up commuting and instead stay at home and let telecommunications take the strain. One commodity dealer, Jeremy Oates, tried staying on his farm at Petersfield but it did not work. His firm's managing director, Christopher Grey-Edwards explains why he now uses his office in EC3:

> If you leave Mincing Lane, you miss the human relationship. Here, you can just pop across the road and do business. You hear things and feel things. It is a personal thing, that third dimension which you do not get if you are doing business from a distance. Telecommunications are fine, and it is possible to conduct business on the telephone, but you miss that third dimension. There are very few people in the commodities business and your relationship with them is all-important. You could play bridge over the telephone, but not poker. The commodities market is like the latter purely because of the importance of the human element.

Shopping

Everyone has their own particular problems with work, housing and travel, but shopping remains a common experience, though the nature of it is also changing. It is unlikely that any developer will quickly follow the example of Hammersons, who took twelve years to get planning permission and build the American-style Brent Cross Centre at the junction of the North Circular Road and M1 extension. The centre looks set for success with two million potential customers within a twenty minute drive. Its marbled halls attract families to picnic in centrally-heated comfort by the fountains. But most developers would not wish to struggle through the planning machine to create another centre only six miles from the West End, unless, perhaps, it is on an open site in Docklands. The trend is more likely to be towards superstores and hypermarkets on the edge of London. Roads are better, sites cheaper, and the suburban family can easily drive out on bulk-buying expeditions.

In London there have been some shopping gains, some losses. Asian families taking over and setting up small supermarkets, then living over the shop, often provide late-night services. But generally, the number of small shops is falling; bigger floor areas are more economical, and in areas like Kensington, boutiques, antique shops and restaurants can boost takings through the tourist trade and afford to pay higher rents than butchers and bakers. As Leonard Reeve-Smith of the National Food and Drink Federation says:

> Small clothes shops are better at surviving than small grocery shops because people do not compare prices of clothes so much. One skirt is not directly comparable to another; whereas there are lots of brand names in food, with every grocery stocking them, so people can make direct comparisons.

Londoners still love the markets of Berwick Street and Brixton, Portobello Road and Mile End. But even there, bric-a-brac and records push out some fruit and vegetable stalls. Not only have the economics changed, but so have the financial realities of being a shopkeeper; he now struggles with stock control and the VAT man, instead of bargaining at wholesale markets and chastising the errand boys. Tommy Matkin, of the Retail Fruit Federation, said:

> A lot of small greengrocers stopped trading because their leases expired and they could not afford to renew them. They were mainly older people and they retired. It used to be a question of them keeping the shop: for the small greengrocers that are left, it is a question of the shop keeping them. A lot of greengrocers were in the business for the fun of it – they got a thrill out of buying because it was very speculative. Now we have a much more sophisticated system, with things pre-packaged and standardised and it is more efficient but less fun. In the old days, it was a way of life – now it is a business.

West End stores have geared themselves up for tourism. Selfridges has eight interpreters on radio links as well as foreign assistants. Like other stores they feel that Westminster Council and the GLC should do their bit to attract visitors by smartening up Oxford Street. Charles Atsma, assistant general manager of Selfridges, said:

> Unless Oxford Street is made a pleasanter place, tourists will stop coming here. We make sure that Selfridges' facade is kept up and in good condition, so we think that Westminster City Council should do their bit in making the street more attractive. I would not want to do away with the buses and taxis here, because it is important to have transport. But you could have multi-coloured paving stones, and prettier trees, budgerigars in bird cages, even. Then look at the bus stops and shelters – so unattractive, just lumps of concrete. There should be telephones around the bus stops – people are often wanting to call home and ask the size of a husband's shirt, or say they have been held up and are on their way. That sort of facility should be on the street. There should be many more litter bins. Continentals like

to drink coca-cola in the street, and if there are no bins the cans are thrown into the street, which is not cleaned often enough. On a Saturday, it is sometimes piled high. We depend on tourists and should make sure we keep them.

The planners in local and central government consider these changes in terms of population shifts, travel patterns and employment statistics. They worry about the changing economic base of the city, and erect local and strategic plans to try and make some order out of the confusion of change. They convince themselves that by setting out some dreams on paper, they will come true. They wait in hopeful expectation that the next census will prove they guessed right.

City of change

But in considering housing, transport and employment policies, it is easy to forget that their purpose is to enhance the quality of individual lives as well as to contribute to the economic well-being of the capital. Too often the individual suffers for what is considered the greater good: economic growth does not guarantee that hardship and deprivation are eliminated; indeed, they may be exacerbated. When there is more money for individuals to spend on housing, it is the poor and elderly who are squeezed out of their homes by the economically strong buying more space. As car ownership increases with higher earnings, those same groups have to wait longer at the bus stop. Immigrant groups who have been deliberately recruited to provide cheap labour in catering and public services have become essential to London's economy, and add to the variety and vitality of many areas. Yet even when the economy is buoyant they have difficulty in securing reasonable housing; when the slump comes they are the first to suffer.

Concentrations of deprivation are more obvious in capital cities, because the unskilled are attracted to low-paid service work, and pressure on housing pushes the poor into the worst conditions. A big city is not a friendly place. Its vastness and anonymity can be chilling for the individual, and its size and diversity makes understanding and direction difficult for the administrator.

A description of the particular problems of these groups and individuals, and the way in which social and related services cope with them, would be the subject of a separate book. Any attempt to analyse all the problems in depth would be pretentious for, as David Plank, research secretary of the Personal Social Services Council points out:

> I don't think there is really anybody who speaks with profound knowledge of London, London's personal circumstances. There might be a few directors who have an overall view, but there isn't

anybody who is responsible for social services in a London sense, because people don't look at it in that way. They look at it as thirty-three social service authorities, thirty-two boroughs and the City.

In 1977 London is in a critical state of transition. The current focus upon inner city problems gives some indication of the concern amongst politicians and planners. The concern is not merely for what will happen. The problems are with us now and are reflected in the disproportionately high burden on London's services, and the spending necessary to maintain them.

In 1976-77 the London boroughs spent on average, in rates and government grant, £32,194 on social services for every thousand residents. Outside London the figures for town districts were £19,810 and for the country only £14,776. The figures for inner boroughs were even higher: Tower Hamlets spent £65,411, Westminster £45,021, and Hackney £51,598.

It is more difficult to be specific about the factors which make London special. A report by the International Hospital Federation published in February 1976 summed up the general feeling:

> Planners in London have to wrestle with the problems caused by the untypical nature of London; its role as the capital city, and its population with its variety of transient, elderly, single, immigrant, commuter, tourist, homeless, rootless and destitute, and the general shift of population from the centre to the periphery.

One aspect which can be identified is the magnetism of the capital city to those with social problems. David Plank believes that:

> London has a certain aura about it. There are all kinds of myths about its opportunities; also it has an anonymity which many people want.

The capital seems to attract, for instance, the alcoholics and the addicts who can get supplies more easily there, the young pregnant girls who can get abortions while sheltering behind the anonymity of the big city, the runaway children who discover that the streets are not paved with gold. This is not a new phenomenon, but nor is it central to the problems. More fundamental is the transitory nature of London's population.

Historically the general picture is of the young middle-class couples and families moving out of inner areas in search of homes with gardens, while the poorer families who remain are supplemented by others who can find no other place to live. These underlying changes have been reinforced by planning policies. Attempts to improve the housing and general environment of inner London have accelerated the trend towards dispersal. Comprehensive development schemes have involved the take-over of much of the private sector and have pushed out settled communities, some who would have preferred to stay. The New and Expanding Towns have provided sites for firms wanting to move from London and relatively inexpensive homes for the young and skilled who followed them. Nick Raynsford, director of SHAC, is exasperated by what has been happening:

> It is crazy. For the last three years the GLC has been pressing, though not very successfully, for a co-ordinated system of allocation in public sector housing in London, yet has presided over its own hopelessly inadequate New and Expanding Towns Scheme. County Hall has resisted all calls which have come from us and other people to establish a properly co-ordinated framework of nomination to New Towns for people in housing need. The explanation is not hard to find. It is basically that the GLC is reluctant to consider any change in its policies on moving out of London, because County Hall is hostile to the concept of anyone moving out of London, and the fear of loss of employment. There is also entrenched defensiveness of the existing machine, and unwillingness to accept that it has broken down, that it is not working, and that it ought really to be completely reorganised. The people who are suffering are the people who are living in rotten conditions, the people who would be willing to move but just don't get the opportunities.

The suburban ideal

Betty Shreeve of the advertising agency Ogilvy Benson & Mather holds group discussions with those families who look for a better life on the edge of London:

> We find it far more useful to think of a population with a top ten per cent of the affluent and culturally aware, twenty per cent of those at the bottom perhaps on social security, and a middle mass of about seventy per cent. The media and central London may be dominated by the top ten per cent, but it is the seventy per cent who determine the political direction of the country and what is sold in the shops. Class distinctions have blurred. The real difference lies on two other dimensions, car ownership and home ownership. The lifestyle of a car-owning family with their own house in the suburbs is very different from that of someone in a council flat relying on public transport in the inner city – but these days they may well both be what was once known as working class. The car and home owning family may be that of a skilled electrician or a university lecturer, and it is quite likely that both will live on an estate on the edge of London. Over the

> past few years, the wages of skilled workers have been beating inflation, while those of the white-collar workers have not, tending to bring the two groups closer together in what they buy and where they live. Increasingly, the husband will drive to work in the suburbs and they will use the car for a big shopping expedition.
>
> Inflation has meant that there is less money for entertainment, and people go to the pub rather than a restaurant. The cinema is mainly for the young – family entertainment is likely to be a drive with the kids in the country. There is an increasing trend to home-based activities, whether it is just watching television, gardening, mending the car, or do-it-yourself repairs to the home. Although there is now a blending of classes, it is a mistake to think that the working classes are taking on middle class cultural values. I don't think the interest in theatre, serious books, music or even high academic standards has ever been the dominant pre-occupation of most people. My experience is that we remain a materially acquisitive society. The families I talk to would put their house and car above everything else – they will cut expenditure elsewhere before jeopardising the mortgage or car. After that they want television sets and freezers. They want to spend their own money, rather than have the council or state spend it for them – and this rather reactionary tendency to form ratepayers' associations or their equivalent is what is drawing Ford workers and professionals together.

It is the search for this sort of lifestyle which has led to the dramatic decline in London's population over the past thirty years, and which has created some of the problems of the inner areas. The single-parent families, the elderly, the unemployed cannot leave for the suburbs. They subsist on social security, are allocated flats on the older council estates where rents are lower, and form ghettos of deprivation and dependency. They cannot afford to buy a home in the suburbs, and the New Towns do not want to be burdened with too many welfare cases. For the poorer families of the inner areas, life is hard. As inflation cuts into income, it becomes more necessary for the mother to go out to work and find somewhere for under-fives to go during the day. Yet as Government squeezes council spending, there is pressure to cut down on nurseries and mothers are forced to employ child-minders.

Old and poor

The elderly can seldom afford to move and are less likely to want to do so because there is not for them the added incentive of finding a job elsewhere and starting a new life. The age problem, as David Plank explains, is not confined to London:

> Nationally, there is going to be a massive increase in the number of elderly people. In particular the over-75 and over-85 age groups are growing at a quite phenomenal rate. We have done one calculation applying the present rate of local authority residential accommodation for the old to the population forecast for 1991. Our estimates show that England and Wales will need an additional 900 forty-bedded homes by 1991. Of course, there may be alternative ways of dealing with the problem but it gives you some idea of the scale of action that is required to deal with very dependent elderly people who can't go on living in their own homes.

Although the general trend is national, the resulting imbalance of population will be accentuated in London. Barbara Spears, Secretary of the Greater London Association for Pre-Retirement, explains:

> There is a pretty clear trend of the general population of London falling and the numbers of elderly, which means the proportion of elderly, rising. There is a clear picture of the parents remaining in the inner city, whereas the young people have been moving out and living in the suburbs. This immediately highlights the problem. If you live in Bromley and your elderly mother lives in Camden, it is practically a day's outing to go and see her.

The poor are also left stranded in the inner city, without the money or skills necessary to enable them to move out in search of better homes and new jobs. In recession, they have no choice but to join the dole queues. The environment has improved, but there have been other losses. Comprehensive development has broken many of the community ties, often replacing overcrowded houses with high rise blocks; where there were twenty streets, now there may be one large impersonal estate.

Education

Some of the problems in the inner areas seem self-perpetuating. For instance, the children are leaving school without the skills or qualifications they need to get a job. There is not a sufficiently-skilled workforce to attract industry and the young cannot afford to move away to find work. Research carried out by the Inner London Education Authority in 1973-1976 concluded that educational standards in inner London were generally lower than the national average. It reported that, for example, applying an educational standard which could be reached by forty per cent of children nationally, in London only twenty-five per cent of children would reach it. Recently tests have shown that in verbal reasoning ability the results for inner London children are improving but in some areas the situation is still particularly bad. Take Newham, for instance, which though an outer London borough as defined in administrative terms, has many characteristics of an inner London borough. In 1974/75 it sent fewer children to university than any other borough in the country and only one child in ten got any 'O' levels, as against a national average of one child in four.

In an attempt to provide a counter-balance to low educational attainment in deprived areas, the Labour Government in 1968 introduced a scheme of 'positive discrimination' by which extra funds are allocated to educational priority areas and stress schools. Of the seven largest grants made in the first phases of the scheme, three were made to areas in London – Islington, Brent and Lambeth. In an article in the *Municipal Services Journal,* Bob Hudson, a lecturer in social studies, explained the rationale of the scheme:

> Essentially it is that poor people in poor areas have needs which are out of the ordinary. They may suffer from the multiple effects of unemployment, poor housing, low income, inferior schools, inadequate community institutions and so forth. Thus city growth creates unusual 'black spots' with such severe problems that they require special treatment. As Jim Callaghan said, when introducing the Urban Aid programme in the Commons on 22 July 1968: 'There remain areas of severe social deprivation in a number of our cities and towns – often scattered in relatively small pockets. They require special help to meet their social needs and to bring their physical services to an adequate level.'

Criticism is levelled at the scheme for adopting the wrong approach. The argument is that the disadvantages of the children involved arise out of community and home environment; as the scheme can help only the school influence, not parental influence, it is of little benefit.

Protagonists believe that the scheme provides the most practical means of improving all those factors. Central Government allocates the extra resources but leaves the schools to decide how best they can be used. That is the point of concern: What approach should the schools adopt, how far should – or can – they take steps to avoid becoming isolated from the communities which they serve? Anne Jones, headmistress of Vauxhall Manor School, explains some of the do's and don'ts:

> I think the greatest thing we have to do is to acknowledge that while the children may have some problems in their backgrounds, it does not follow that they have problems in themselves. We should also be careful not to adopt the approach of thinking that we cannot expect much of the children because they have got difficulties. I think schools have a right and a responsibility to make more demands on their pupils. If you don't expect anything, all you do in fact is denigrate students. If

you expect them to do something, you are implying an expectation that they have some ability, whatever it might be.

I think many parents' attitude reflects the kind of education they had themselves. They often just expect higher standards in the three Rs and firm discipline. The problem is how to keep the humane aspects of caring and showing concern at the same time as making demands and getting higher standards of achievement. We have found that the more we have done this, the more positive the children have been about learning.

We are very much against the old academic approach that puts the intelligent student out on a limb and then denies the value of the other student. I think at one point we may have swept out the academic achievement in an attempt to be egalitarian. We should try to recognise achievement but not make that the only criteria . . . The children all know who the brighter ones are, and those that are brighter must learn not to have to be patted on the head just because they are lucky enough to be bright.

Better links between home and school have had some success. Sue Newman, a co-ordinator of Social Services in Lambeth, gave the example of a local comprehensive school which a few years ago attracted considerable attention from the media:

There is now much less violence, higher attainment, and, it seems, more interest amongst pupils. I believe these results have been achieved by a change in attitude and approach: more real involvement of staff, smaller classes, taking out kids for individual tuition, gearing things to individual needs to some extent, development of the counselling role with individual kids; trying to do something in linking up school with home and making it that much more real to the families. There is now a social worker based at the school. That couldn't have been contemplated a few years ago; it would not have occurred either to the school or to the Social Services. Their approach has broadened.

Some schools make great efforts to base in the school things that will appeal to the families – socials and dances. A lot of them are very well attended, but it requires a tremendous amount of effort on the part of the school staff. Nevertheless, it is seen as important to those who think of the school as some sort of community provision and it is slowly becoming a more widely accepted approach; but it depends on the nature of the head. A lot of them believe that the school is not just for the school kids, but is also for the community to use. Nevertheless, many schools would be very resistant to having the social services involved because they feel very threatened by anything that questions their institutional basis.

Community involvement

However there are signs of a new approach towards more community involvement, less isolation. Similar trends are apparent throughout the services. There is a general concern at the way in which efforts aimed at improving efficiency have sacrificed many aspects of personal involvement with the community. For instance in the police force it has meant a shift away from the Bobby on the beat. Chief Inspector John Newing explains:

> The escalation of 'mobile crime' has increased the need for the use of cars as the method of patrolling. Panda cars constitute the police force's response to events and this has led to the partial demise of the man on the beat. Since the late 1960s continuing efforts have been made to restore the balance.
>
> We recognise that it is mainly through the local Bobbies that we become involved in the community. Their advantage is that they are not associated by the passers-by with wrong doing. You can talk to them; you can't pass the time of day with a panda car.

Similarly, the decline of local doctors is seen by the medical profession as the most worrying aspect of London's health service. An International Hospital Federation survey in 1976 reported that the problems of general practice in London were mentioned more often than any other topic except that of the new NHS structure:

> Comments about the relatively low quality of many inner city general practices were matched by those that questioned whether the conventional pattern of the family doctor style of general practice is appropriate through a big city. Likewise comments about primary care being left to the hospitals without them being explicitly geared to the task were matched by those that argued that the ready availability of these hospital services encouraged the atrophy of GP skills.

For the social services, the areas of concern are not easily identified and solutions less clear-cut. Certainly there have been moves towards greater involvement in the community. Since 1976, David Ennals, DHSS Secretary, has been pressing for greater emphasis upon intermediate treatment of juvenile offenders through community-based services, rather than putting the children into residential homes. In other areas, the moves to integrate social services within the community are well under way. Nevertheless, the frustration felt by many social workers is understandable: they are seldom in a position which enables them to have a fundamental effect. Sue Newman explains:

> I think either people tend to keep themselves to themselves until driven to absolute desperation, by which time our course of action is very limited because the events have forced a certain

sort of action on us; or else people do not refer themselves direct. We are alerted by some other agent, the school or GP . . . It sometimes seems a self-defeating exercise because we feel as if we are under siege; like a fire brigade service, only called upon when some disaster has occurred. It is not satisfying to work in that sort of set-up at all. And yet to some extent we create the situation for ourselves by saying that we can't take on what we call preventative work, which is really the interesting, productive area where maybe one would have the opportunity to influence people whose lives are rather depressing. If you took all those social services and added up how much they spend it would be astronomical, and yet we know very little about the effects of this expenditure and whether it would not be better spent earlier than later.

Whatever the arguments about the distribution of resources within the social services, one point is clear: the provision of resources to the social service departments of the London boroughs rose by over 400 per cent between 1965 and 1975 (from £30 million to £154 million), far more than average earnings on the retail price index.

The relative jump in expenditure is to a large extent attributable to higher social aspirations – a growing awareness of the community's obligations to its more deprived members. Sue Newman explains:

> One's perspective keeps on changing as society's expectations change. For example, look at what we mean by being homeless: at one time if young people wanted to start a family, they would live with in-laws or something – the expectation now is that they will get a flat and, unless they do, they are often considered homeless. Councils, in reflecting the views of society, need to respond to this; so that sort of problem may seem to be getting worse. Equally we have more battered children cases brought to us, because of the publicity given to that problem and because of society's expectations that someone will do something about it.

These changes, as Sue Newman was careful to point out, are welcome. The factors to which she draws attention are first, that the problems are not always getting worse, but rather we are more aware of them, and secondly, that the social services are finding it difficult to keep up with these rising aspirations because they do not have the resources to cope with the growing pressures upon them. As David Plank observed:

> Where social service provision is made, so need appears and demand is infinite: In effect, for instance, the more social workers there are the more problems they will find. The state cannot provide comprehensive care for all the ills of society, it is a physical impossibility; you have to have some kind of

manufacturing base. If the public services continued to grow as they have recently, it wouldn't be very long before everybody was employed in them, and that is not a situation that can exist. One needs an economic base.

Scarce resources

That is the crux of the problem. The expenditure cuts indicate that for the foreseeable future there is likely to be little room for manoeuvre and almost none for overall expansion. Therefore the crucial question is how best to allocate and distribute the resources available. It is true that in London there will be less children to care for, but there will be more old people. In addition, as David Plank points out:

> With the falling child population you would expect the children-in-care population to decline, but it hasn't because although the number coming into care has decreased, the number of children staying in care for a longer period of time has increased. So there is a reduced turn-over of those children, but an increasing children-in-care population.
>
> One certainty is that the social problems will not go away just because expenditure has been cut. Given that social problems are greater in London than elsewhere, the authorities in Greater London are going to be under very severe pressure. People who would have received services in the past, won't in future; there may well be a switch of effort from statutory resources to self-help and voluntary activities, which I believe is a good thing as we are too dependent on official care services – we must face up to the fact that the statutory services will not be able to keep pace with demand in almost any area.

Sue Newman believes that there is potential for making better use of school buildings:

> Most of these expensive buildings are closed each week day from 4 pm and completely at week-ends and in holidays. We aren't making enough use of them, like a lot of municipal buildings.

Bev Woodroffe thinks that with the fall in number of schoolchildren, a more flexible approach is being adopted towards the use of schools:

> Educational planners are changing their thinking somewhat. They realise that we have a massive number of primary schools which are three storey buildings. The school population will only be enough to use two storeys so the planners are thinking about how the extra space will be used. There will be some rationalisation of teachers' centres, and other sorts of support units brought into schools. The fact that they move into school

may change the way in which they function. The teachers' centres may relate their development much more closely to the school in which they are housed and to the neighbourhood in general.

In some areas of education, however, there are pressing problems which can only be resolved by use of more resources. A particular problem for inner areas of London is that unemployment is unlikely to be substantially reduced unless there is available a larger pool of skilled workers than at present – otherwise industry will not be able to recruit the type of labour it wants. Anne Jones spells out the problem:

> I think it is important to get a more coherent understanding of what the schools are trying to do and of what the parents expect the school to do and what people after school, particularly the employers, expect and want from school children. I think there is a great deal to be done on improving the transition from school to work and the links with the community. This is something we are just beginning to battle with. Some of my colleagues and I are going to meet a group of employers and discuss what type of maths they expect, what kind of maths we do and why there appears to be a discrepancy. Schools are failing to examine not so much the type of knowledge but rather the kind of skill and the approach to work which could actually be useful to the children. We need to explore these questions much more than we are doing.

But more immediately, there is an urgent need for better training facilities. As Tom Rees says:

> There then arises the question of how to make young people 'employable' when they aren't used to working and they have no experience of work. There is a big job for the state agencies, the Training Services agency, for the local authorities and the ILEA to run preparation for work courses and second-chance training courses – invent any name you like to make them sound attractive. Not only is it important for them to teach the basic reading and writing skills, they must also teach the children how to present themselves, how to dress, how to talk to people on the telephone, that they must turn up punctually for work, learn to be polite to their supervisors and all that kind of thing.

There are of course many other problems which are likely to get worse. Many of London's services suffer from shortage and rapid turnover of staff. Hospital cuts will be substantial in London; many voluntary services that need grants from Government to keep going are in danger of closing down. The difficulties are more severe because the momentum of growth in the past must be checked and that presents special problems. David Plank:

> The inbuilt growth rate is such that in order to bring it down to the ceiling which is required in the current cash limit situation, certain projects will not take place, and others will not be commissioned. It is happening in the social services, in the personal social services, and in the health service. It is bound to happen because the capital programme projects take at least three years from start to finish. The level of capital programme which was being started three years ago was high because the level of public expenditure was growing at a very fast rate. Now one main way in which to cut that off is by stopping the schemes and leaving the buildings empty.

But whatever the problems, it is necessary to put London in perspective. Britain and London benefit from one of the most comprehensive social welfare systems in the world. Other services like housing, transport, shopping and entertainment facilities are far more advanced than in most other countries and accessible to a far greater proportion of the population.

The report of the survey on London's health services carried out by the International Hospital Federation commented that:

> Respondents referred to the high standards of the basic environmental and public health services of London – sanitation, water supply, clean air, parks, etc. These are all factors which one tends to take for granted here, but which are still the source of major problems in many other big cities particularly in the developing world.

Nevertheless, there is still a lot of room for improvement; the IHF report concluded:

> A wide variety of other good ideas and practices were mentioned in fields such as housing, transport, nutrition, community development schemes, youth services and voluntary help. Many of these topics had also been mentioned in the problems' section of the questionnaire as being areas of activity where too little was being done, which gives a good indication of the potential for improving the situation in London.

Community action

One should not be too gloomy. The street parties, concerts and fireworks of Jubilee Year celebrations are giving an uplift to flagging morale, and Jubilee projects are catching some of the spirit of community action and self-help which is returning to London. Appropriately, funds raised for the celebrations have provided a new park on the south bank site of the Festival of Britain, which helped launch the confidence of the 1950s. Local groups have tackled derelict sites and buildings in Paddington and Clerkenwell, Newham and the Isle of Dogs – old warehouses are being turned into workshops, urban farms are being created and playgrounds laid out. One scheme, in Clerkenwell, shows how much can be achieved with sufficient drive and some help from local councils. In 1975, Mike Franks left his job with the GLC, where he was a member of the Covent Garden planning team, and helped to start an operation to convert an old warehouse into small workshops. The owners of the building, the GLC, granted a short lease, and conversion and improvement work was done to minimum standards on limited funds. There are now 200 tenants, and a stream of applicants for space in Clerkenwell workshops. Mr Franks concludes that councils must give up their arrogant belief that they are the only agency for controlling the way land must be developed – they must talk to the small firms or local groups who could use empty sites and buildings:

> Local authorities must de-mystify the property game and promote the continual use of the built environment instead of blighting hundreds of acres with their grand conceptions. Empty space is a form of urban cancer, but it can be cured. Councils should encourage groups of small firms to form co-operatives, and then help them find suitable property. The council has all the professional expertise necessary and could help in providing finance or guarantees. Conversion and renovation costs can be kept down if building regulations are rationalised.

Five years' ago community action meant fighting private developers or the local council; with both bureaucracy and big business now broke, talents are turning to community development. However, enthusiasm is not enough, and Government job creation programme funds do not last long. The property slump has meant that many charities have suffered a cut in revenue and cannot give as much support to voluntary bodies; so just when Ministers are preaching the virtues of self-help, the community workers are finding their budgets cut as badly as those of council departments.

Even if more funds are provided to stimulate self-help organisations, it would be over-optimistic to see this as the main force which will regenerate London. A capital city cannot be treated as a rural commune, it is inevitably caught in the grip of international finance, charged and depleted by a flow of visitors and migrants, and ensnared by the transport system which helped create it. Local initiatives will only succeed if they draw on the social and economic forces surging through the urban system. That will mean a new attitude on the part of planners and politicians, who must find ways to harness those forces – or at least the ones they can control –together with the small-scale energy and initiative which is beginning to regenerate some aspects of London. It will mean, too, that planners, politicians and public alike must fight to put more humanity into the planning process, so that it relates as never before to the needs and wishes of the ordinary people of London. A good start would be to complement their statistical analysis with more first-hand perceptions of those needs, wishes, aspirations and fears, some of which are exampled in this book.

Suggested reading

London 1808-1870: The Infernal Wen, Francis Sheppard (Secker and Warburg 1971)
The Symmetrical Family, Young and Willmott (Routledge and Kegan Paul 1973)
See also *Social Trends* (Annual publication of the Government Statistical Service HMSO)
Living in Southwark, Patricia Prescott-Clarke and Barry Hedges of the Social Community Planning Research Centre (London Borough of Southwark 1976)
As They See It, A Race Relations Study of Three Areas from a Black Viewpoint, Lionel Morrison (Community Relations Commission 1976)
Strategy and style in local community relations, Anthony Barker (Runnymede Trust 1975)
Social Problems in Modern Britain, edited by David Weir and Eric Butterworth (Collins/Fontana 1974)
Architecture, Planning and Urban Crime, the report on a Conference organised by NACRO, December 1974 (Obtainable from NACRO – the National Association for the Care and Rehabilitation of Offenders)

MANIFESTO FOR LONDON

This book has examined two of the major forces which determine the future of London. First, the individual decisions of people and firms on how they earn a living and spend their rewards, and where they set up home, factory or office. Secondly, how central and local government try to push and pull these trends by spending our money on roads and housing, or refusing to allow buildings to be erected, cars driven freely, or homes let as landlords wish.

Politicians attempt to reconcile the two at elections, when they are obliged to consider whether their policies are in line with public sentiment. Greater London Council elections, like that of May 1977, should give voters the chance to express their choice of a London moulded by Sir Reg Goodwin or Mr Horace Cutler, instead of by Mr Callaghan or Mrs Thatcher. To put it crudely, voting should be on whether London needs more factories and council houses, or home owners and offices, rather than on who will best deal with inflation.

In practice things do not work out like that. Borough and GLC elections are won or lost, not on local issues, but on the standing of political parties nationally. Over the years most voters have formed some opinion on whether they see their interests best served by Socialism or Conservatism, but they find it hard to discern how their lives will be affected by political decisions of County Hall or Town Hall. So they vote by party colour rather than local policy. Manifestos make little difference to the outcome. Very few voters read them. However, they are important because after the election they become holy writ for the administration in power, at least for the first year while party faithful and conference are assured that their proposals are being implemented.

For this reason, if no other, the planning of London's future must be seen through the proposals of the political parties as well as technical analysis of civil servants and council officers. Manifestos are written to try and catch the current enthusiasms of an electorate, usually as reflected in the media. Labour's attitude to ringways in

1973 and the fact that the Tories dropped any major road proposals from their manifesto of 1977 are classic instances. The motorways have been abandoned more because they are reckoned an electoral disadvantage than because of any profound analysis of the importance or otherwise of better roads. Similarly, one suspects that the parties are plugging the River Line through Docklands merely as an enticing bauble, a demonstration that County Hall can make some mark on the landscape. The project doesn't stand up to close economic scrutiny but, like Concorde, it has some potent charm for politicians. None of this would matter much if manifestos were discarded once the election was won or lost. What does happen is something rather more serious. The election is won on national policies, but the councillors must believe, for their own self-esteem, that voters want them to carry out their local manifesto policies. The electorate is saddled with a policy package they never really voted for. This analysis is not intended as an argument against manifestos, but for a higher level of debate on strategic issues, leading to better policy proposals.

In 1977 it was inevitable that Labour should be on the defensive, proclaiming hopefully on the cover of their manifesto for London that 'It's looking good', despite the slump, but unable to muster anything of greater strategic significance for the cover than an elderly couple rather sheepishly displaying their free bus pass. Sir Reg told the voters that Labour had turned the GLC 'from an organisation which threatened to obliterate London in an orgy of road building and demolition under the Tories to an organisation which is now in the vanguard of inner city rehabilitation'. He did not, of course, remind the voters that it was Labour that first proposed the despised motorway plans in 1965. As evidence of inner city regeneration he trotted out Covent Garden, Piccadilly Circus and Leicester Square; each well within central London. The rest of the message boasted of how much Labour had spent on building homes and keeping fares down. After four years in charge of planning for Docklands the greatest achievement Sir Reg could point to was 1,000 homes in the pipe line and a major land drainage scheme.

In the main body of the twenty-eight page manifesto there was no lack of detail, although more was on past policies than on the future. Labour recalled that it had reversed the policy of encouraging young people to move to the New Towns, it had sought the abolition of the Location of Offices Bureau, and proposed the establishment of an Industrial Development Agency. The Docklands strategy was outlined, with emphasis on council housing and industry, and the need to construct the new River Line tube. The main transport policies were to continue keeping fare increases down through subsidies, to improve services, the aim to transfer freight to rail or water, and to gain more control over British Rail services, taxis and hire cars. In the housing section there was a brief reference to a strategic plan; the traditional emphasis on council house building and improvement; and a puzzling allusion to Labour having stopped the construction of tower blocks – when that had already been done by the Tories, prior to 1973. Apart from the suggestion for a cheap centralised estate agency, most of the section could have been written for a borough council election. Nowhere in the twenty eight pages was there a positive reference to London's two areas of growth, office employment and tourism.

At the time of writing, the final text of the Conservative manifesto is not available, but the policy lines have been made clear to me by Mr Cutler and his colleagues. Like Labour, the Tories say they are determined to press ahead with the redevelopment of Docklands, including the new tube. Mr Cutler, who is a better hand at political gimmicks than Sir Reg, proposes to call it the Jubilee Line. His disposition in Docklands is to repeat the St Katharine Docks exercise, whereby the GLC purchases land, sets out a planning brief, then invites private developers to present detailed proposals. In this way the Tories hope to agree with the boroughs on mixed commercial and housing schemes where at least half the homes would be for sale, and most would have gardens. In housing generally there will be emphasis on renovation in inner London, help for co-operatives, co-ownership schemes, housing associations, home ownership, and any other flexible form of provision not under the direct control of the local authority. The aim will be to help young people to live in London by letting off to them more old council flats and encouraging new developments to cater for small households. Some of the GLC housing estates are to be transferred to the boroughs and there will be a major push to sell council houses at a discount.

Transport policy is to reorganise bus routes to avoid duplication with tube and BR lines, place great emphasis on increasing efficiency to save money, invest in capital improvements, but cut subsidies and put up fares. Roads will be built where there is a strong need or local demand, but the Tories, like Labour, have dropped major schemes for the time being. Mr Cutler also promises to avoid rate increases, cut bureaucratic interference and the duplication of planning powers with the boroughs, and launch an inquiry into the role of the GLC.

The Tories usually produce brief bland manifestos which say so little they are difficult to criticise. However, some major flaws are evident even in the broad outline. The emphasis on the inner city is deceptive. Without corresponding measures to enable poorer families to escape from the housing trap and the unemployment described by Shankland Cox in areas like Stockwell, little will be gained. Labour believes rather unrealistically that industry can be re-established in these areas, and that for this reason the unskilled should stay. The Tories, on the other hand, neither believe that industry should be re-established, nor do they propose any way in which inner city families could move to outer London. In general, the Tory refusal to have anything to do with council housing in outer London, or with substantial transfers between boroughs on a common allocation basis, leaves them without a credible housing strategy of any sort. If a Tory GLC hands over most of its estates to borough control, without retaining power to nominate tenants, there will be no way in which outer London can be obliged to help relieve the stresses of the inner area. The Tory transport policy is open to other objections. If transport subsidies are cut back too quickly, the higher fares could jeopardise employment in central London.

The problems of selling council houses have already been mentioned: most tenants cannot afford to buy except at enormous discounts; only the best homes are sold; and the council loses the capability to relet to those in need.

Of course, it is easy to criticise but more difficult to produce a coherent policy package. But at the risk of parading a package just as leaky as the Tory or Labour proposals, here are some policy conclusions that are drawn from the analysis in preceding chapters.

On one point I agree wholeheartedly with Horace Cutler. After twelve years of ill-defined existence there is an urgent need to establish, at last, an appropriate role for the GLC. There is far too much overlap with boroughs in housing management and in minor traffic matters and in the vetting of planning permissions. The rent collection and maintenance of GLC housing estates could, for example, be handed over to the boroughs, if they were prepared to take on the rather onerous responsibility. The question is what positive role the GLC should adopt at a strategic level.

First of all, I feel three broad principles should be established. The outward movement of people and jobs is likely to continue: what is important is who leaves, how fast the capital spreads, and where the new homes are built. Second, arguments about council housing versus owner-occupation, private versus public transport, offices or industry should be recast. In each instance there is a complementary need for both; it is a case of horses for courses. Not everyone can afford to own a house – or even wishes to. Cars are useful in the suburbs, public transport is best for commuting to the centre and essential even for members of car owning households. Offices operate well in the centre, heavy industry better on the outskirts of towns. The third principle follows: central, inner and outer London are best suited to different activities. On the basis of those three principles, a manifesto on the key issues of employment, housing and transport might be summarised as follows.

Central London is currently losing jobs, yet some firms want to start operations or expand there. Provided they do not want to knock down high-grade historic building or houses, that their activities don't generate a great deal of traffic and they put up well designed buildings, they should not be blocked by planners. There should not be tight controls on offices and hotels, studios, workshops, showrooms or other businesses which can pay the going rent and rates. However, major developments should be concentrated near stations, and some stations rebuilt so that any profits from redevelopment can be ploughed into modernisation and better interchange facilities between buses, tubes and trains. This relaxation of controls and new development would relieve some of the pressure on existing buildings, where small offices and workshops may be threatened with displacement by firms prepared to pay more. Where these essential small-scale activities are jeopardised the GLC and boroughs could use areas where they have holdings more wisely than they do now. Where the council is a major property owner it can act like the large estates, as Grosvenor and the Crown have done in the past, setting profitable schemes against the less profitable. If an office development is allowed on one part of a council land holding, it could pay a cross-subsidy to allow cheaper premises let by the council elsewhere. The mistake in Covent Garden, for instance, lies not in encouraging some workshops – but in failing to realise the other more commercial opportunities the area offers. Furthermore, councils have extensive planning powers which allow them to inhibit development in areas where they wish to resist major change.

On the edge of central London there is scope for encouraging development of station sites like West Hampstead, where a substantial number of lines converge, and could feed in commuters from a wide area without increasing congestion and provide a much-needed boost to local employment. The GLC should stop dragging its heels over the Hammersmith roundabout site and allow the office development which would enable London Transport to build a new bus garage and tube station and to carry out other improvements. The policy of encouraging development of suburban centres should be continued, although more thought should be given to local road improvements and better bus services so that workers and shoppers in neighbouring areas could use them easily.

Major new industrial development in inner London should be concentrated in Docklands, where there is room for expansion, the prospect of better roads linked to the motorway network, and a chance to provide homes for skilled workers. Elsewhere in the inner city small firms and co-operatives wishing to start up should be given advantageous leases on council-owned property, industrial mortgages and waivers on building regulations where appropriate.

Councils should not be over-optimistic about the prospects for a substantial increase in large-scale factory employment. The emphasis should be mainly on keeping what there is already, which will mean changes in housing and transport policy.

Transport policy will be difficult because of the lack of funds. The GLC should consider both the needs of firms and workers, and the social requirements of both car drivers and users of public transport. Increased car ownership, the need to help freight movement, and the need to link with suburban centres suggest some road building is essential in the long term. This does not mean resurrecting the ringways: some dual two-lane roads could be built in the suburbs without too much disruption and junctions could be unlocked by lightweight flyovers like the one at the Hogarth roundabout on the A4. Some little used rail lines might be converted to roads, perhaps for the exclusive use of buses in peak hours. The aim of transport and planning policy should be to maintain the viability of central London, and to ensure that development elsewhere is concentrated into centres which can be well served by public transport. In central London this will mean caution over two policies – fare rises and traffic restraint. Any fare rises should be gradual to avoid a sudden burden on commuters and firms which would give firms an added push outwards, thus increasing car commuting in the suburbs and transport problems generally in the long term. Great care should be taken in introducing extra restraint measures because of the possible damage to firms in the central area. An attack on existing private car parking under office blocks would be unwise because it would be extremely difficult to enforce and not yield proportionate benefit. The effect of past parking controls on commuters has, for example, shifted the problem for buses away from the former peaks of congestion to midday, when through traffic is at its height. The only way to cut out this traffic would be area control, perhaps by special licences.

In the suburbs, each office and shopping centre should be treated more like a small town. A balance must be struck between clearing traffic from shopping streets – by building relief roads and introducing controls, facilities for car parking on the fringe of the centre – and better public transport services. Apart from improving public transport to the suburban centres, some cuts in bus services in outer London, together with fare increases, are inevitable. Without these economies subsidies will continue to swallow funds which could be used to bring essential improvements elsewhere. Some compensation should be provided through encouragement of car sharing, taxi and mini-cab services, and licences for private enterprise bus services.

However, any doctrinaire attempts to make London Transport pay its way within three or four years should be abandoned because they could cause lasting damage. Instead, the level of subsidies should be tailored to ensure that it is possible to run essential social services for those without cars, a basic network to provide access effectively to anywhere in London at predictable frequency, topped up by a good commercial service arranged to pick up as many tourists and commuters as possible. All these services would, of course, be part of the same network. The point is that policy makers should be precise about why they are giving subsidies, and who they are benefiting. Even the toughest policy should not aim to do more than halve the London Transport subsidy in two or three years. Although the GLC can hardly expect to gain control of British Rail services in the short term, some overall consideration of policy is necessary. There is more than a suspicion that British Rail station manning and investment levels in local lines may be over generous, and could be better used elsewhere in the transport network.

Housing policy is impossible to resolve until the Government makes up its mind about finance. The present system is chaotic, and helps ensure that some are very well housed for relatively little outlay, while others cannot get a roof over their heads. Owner-occupiers are faced with heavy outgoings when they take on a mortgage, but the burden reduces as wages rise and payments stay much the same. The council tenant may have an easier start, but rents generally rise with wages, and the tenant has no stake in the property. The private tenant and private landlord both do badly because they are subsidised less. The present system of tax relief encourages home owners to trade up to better property as soon as they can afford to, since they get more relief on the new borrowing. The result is a tendency to over-consumption of housing.

Broad housing policy should be to keep alive the private landlord, to give selective encouragement to owner-occupation; and to keep the benefits of council housing by not disposing of property rashly. These three policy aims can be pursued without contradiction by encouraging each in a different area. The private landlord is particularly important in central London, because that is where the young and mobile want to rent rather than buy. More council housing is needed in outer London to decant inner London families to better conditions; this may not involve just new building since there are plenty of semi-detached homes which could be bought more cheaply than councils can build. At the same time there should be some encouragement for owner occupation in inner London, where families may be prepared to buy and improve property more cheaply than councils. If necessary, councils should buy property, rehouse tenants and then sell on, offering mortgages and grants. In this way they should help reshuffle small households into flats, and families into houses with gardens.

An agreed housing strategy for London is essential if these changes are to be achieved. At present the GLC, central Government and boroughs pull in different directions. If the GLC cannot – or will not – reach agreement with the boroughs then the Department of the Environment must knock some heads together. It has the instrument in its new system for allocating funds: if a borough refuses to join in a common system for allocating council houses fairly across London, or won't meet targets for renovation and building, then the Government can hold back subsidies. There will be no easing of London's housing problems unless there is a programme of action which has some hope of lasting beyond the next set of elections. Intervention by central Government would run against the tendency to allow more local decision making – but in London there seems no other option unless the two parties at County Hall can find some common ground and consequently make a case for the GLC having greater powers.

There is no shortage of specific proposals to fit within a strategic framework. Experiments with tenants' co-operatives, co-ownership schemes whereby groups can get joint mortgages, part-rent and part-buy schemes should all be encouraged, although most will make only marginal contributions. More funds should be diverted into council mortgages for the inner city, or some form of guarantee agreed which would enable building societies to lend. More old council estates and tower blocks unsuitable for families should be let to young people. Councils and housing associations should consider letting some of their property on a market basis, at higher rents, to provide some substitute for the private landlord. There is no one-shot solution to London's housing problems, but there are two prerequisites for specific proposals: a long-term strategy, and far more concern to ensure that the appropriate policies are pursued in the right place.

Inevitably, Docklands will be a testing ground for fresh ideas. Labour has made the mistake of producing a strategy which is totally inconsistent: it proposes a tube line and industry, when the most appropriate way of using the River Line – were it built – would be to put offices above the stations and build homes for sale to City workers. Factories need roads. The Tories are more consistent, but equally deluded in believing that the tube should be built. If £200 million is available, there are better ways to spend it. Their enthusiasm for home ownership could be disastrous if all the best riverside sites go to private developers, and council estates are built without nearby jobs, with an attractive environment and good bus services. The homes will be refused by those tenants who can afford to be choosy, and the estates will become dumping grounds for poorer homeless families.

Both parties should instead shift their concern from the River Line and concentrate on construction of the East London River Crossing – a bridge or tunnel – at the eastern end of Dockland which would link up to the North Circular road, and south to the A2. This would do more than anything else to bring industry to the area and to north east London providing a real gateway to Europe for industrialists. To encourage industrialists it might be necessary to allocate some of the new council housing specifically to individual firms, so that skilled workers could be assured of homes as they are in the New Towns. Overall, the GLC should concentrate on improving roads, sewers and drainage, then parcel up areas for competition among developers. The council would buy land and keep the freehold, set out a design brief, and take the best offer on the lines established in St Katharine and London Docks.

The failure of Trammell Crow to take up 130 acres in Surrey Docks has left a vacuum south of the river. Some major generator of jobs and economic activity is needed there, or perhaps north of the Thames on the Isle of Dogs. One possibility is an English variation of Disneyland, a leisure and recreation complex which could offer everything from a super funfair to exhibition and sports halls. In the United States, these parks, occupying several hundred acres, each provide work for about 1,200 people, ranging from cleaners and catering staff, to skilled engineers and electricians to maintain and rebuild constantly changing displays. The tourist potential would be tremendous, and the spin-off for local people in jobs, shopping and recreation facilities would be considerable.

In Docklands, as in all the major policy areas, nothing will be achieved unless there is the chance of a proposal surviving the next election. It is bad enough for central Government policy to change every few years, throwing housing, transport and planning programmes back and forth. When borough and GLC elections intervene as well, stalemate is guaranteed. As I argued earlier, there is a strong case to be made for keeping the GLC in some leaner form. On the other hand it seems unlikely that transport and housing policies will be carried through without some firmer direction from the Government departments concerned. One wishes the GLC were smaller and more effective – but fears that without the sanction of Government intervention that would simply lead to more protracted disputes within the boroughs. I hope this book has indicated how unintentionally damaging many good intentions of planners and politicians have been, and how likely it is that the present unco-ordinated system and the party stances will continue to perpetuate the mistakes of the past. Calling for the abolition of the GLC or an end to party politics in the council chamber dodges the issue that London must be representatively governed at a strategic level, and that most of the issues are supremely political. I cannot propose any resolution of such a knotty constitutional issue, but I hope that as the residents of London pack their belongings for the great march to the suburbs and beyond, the rustle of discontent will penetrate the complacency of County Hall and Westminster.

ACKNOWLEDGMENTS

This book could not have been written without the assistance of a large number of people and organisations. My particular thanks are due to David Richards, who gathered and organised a great deal of detailed information, and helped to structure the chapters and to write several of them.

The entire project was sponsored by Thames Television who achieved the difficult balance between maximum support and minimum interference.

The Greater London Council has, through its successes and failures, been the inspiration for many of the ideas in the book; its officers and members have been consistently helpful although they knew that the result was likely in some ways to be critical of their work. We are deeply indebted to the Policy Studies and Intelligence Branch and the Research Library.

Although the GLC figures most prominently, this was not intended to imply any less regard for London's borough councils. Many council leaders supplied detailed analyses of their boroughs and the developments they foresaw over the next 15 years and I am sorry that lack of space prevented a fuller exposition of their thoughts.

Officers of the Department of the Environment, Department of Transport, London Transport, British Rail, Central London Planning Conference, and the Standing Conference on London and South East Regional Planning have helped at various points.

Much of the material in the book resulted from seven years reporting for the Evening Standard, and I am grateful for additional assistance from the library staff there.

Dr David Copsey was particularly helpful on the transport chapter, and I would like to thank Malcolm Allan, Alan Duguid, Bernard Crofton, Bernard Kilroy, and David Webster for their considerable help on the housing chapter.

The Shankland Cox Partnership provided many of the ideas for the inner city section, and officers of Bexley council prompted many of the thoughts on suburbs.

Thanks to everyone we spoke to in the course of our research, in particular Fred Baker, John Bosman, Charles Boxer, Alan Cryer, Bill D'Arcy, David Hencke, Joe Hirsh, Anne Jones, Tony Judge, Tommy Macpherson, Sue

Newman, John O'Brien, David Plank, Usha Prashar, Nick Raynsford, Tom Rees, Betty Shreeve, Geoffrey Smith, Barbara Spears, Bev Woodroffe.

Typing the drafts, which required a considerable ability to cope with frequent revisions as well as great stamina, was accomplished by Anne Macgregor, Ruth Stockwell and Jennifer Norton, who also gathered much of the information for the maps and diagrams.

My wife Judy displayed equal stamina in doing her own job, looking after Daniel, and keeping us both sane during the final panic of production.